# HOW
### TO
## ⚬⚬ TIE ⚬⚬
# KNOTS

First published in Great Britain in 2020 by Modern Books
An imprint of Elwin Street Productions Limited
14 Clerkenwell Green
London EC1R 0DP
www.modern-books.com

ISBN: 978-1-912827-48-0

10 9 8 7 6 5 4 3 2 1

Printed in China

# HOW
## TO
# 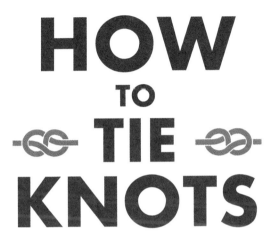 TIE
# KNOTS

**Tim MacWelch**

# CONTENTS

**INTRODUCTION**

## 01

**KNOTS YOU NEED
TO KNOW**

## 02

**CAMPING AND
HIKING KNOTS**

## 03

**NAUTICAL KNOTS**

## CLIMBING KNOTS

## FISHING KNOTS

# WHY YOU NEED KNOTS

Most of us tie knots every day. We might tie our shoelaces, the top of a bag of rubbish, a necktie, a dog lead, a ribbon or a length of sewing thread, and we typically perform these actions without thinking. Our fingers go through the motions, just as they have done a thousand times before. But how often do you stop to consider the intricate skill set you are using?

Knot tying has always been an essential skill, whether for fishing, camping, climbing or travelling across water. Developed by our ancestors, many knots date back beyond recorded history and have been passed down through the generations. Even in modern times, we continue to tie knots despite the invention of Velcro, metal snaps, duct tape, superglue and a host of other contemporary fasteners. For certain jobs, it's hard to rival the simple efficiency of tying the right knot in the right piece of cordage.

While most people know how to tie two or three basic knots, some of us have a large repertoire of knots at our disposal and understand just how critical it can be to tie the right one. Knots are part of a tool kit for self-reliance, and you need to have a firm 'handle' on the right one to do each task safely and effectively. Ask an angler how they would make their catch without their favourite netmaking and angling knots. Ask a firefighter or rock climber how important a knot can be when someone's life is literally hanging in the balance. Even in our 'space age' times, the age-old skill of knot tying remains an indispensable tool to those who provide for themselves, protect others and venture into the mountains or out at sea.

There are hidden benefits, too. Whether you are a youngster or have years of experience, learning to tie new knots can increase your hand–eye coordination and help you develop problem-solving skills. Knot tying also builds strong fingers, creativity and greater self-reliance. And who knows when your knot-tying skills might save the day? The best part is that anyone can do it. In this book, you'll learn how to tie knots that have many day-to-day applications. You'll also discover knots that are useful during outdoor activities (such as camping, climbing, sailing and fishing). You'll even learn how to use rope to create and build. Just pay attention to the details, focus on learning one knot at a time and have fun with it. You never know when your new knot-tying knowledge will come in handy.

Even though you might be able to muddle through life knowing only a few knots, it's a far better plan to learn (and practise) as many knots as possible. The more knots you know, the more options you have in your day-to-day activities as well as in emergency settings. Learn these knots well, make sure you take some rope on your next adventure and you'll be even better prepared to face the challenges that lie ahead.

Best of luck and happy knot tying,


Tim MacWelch

# CHOOSING A ROPE

There are as many kinds of ropes, lines, cords and strings available today as there are knots to tie in them. The most important thing is always to select the right rope for the job, and tie an appropriate knot in it. While some ropes and materials will accept any knot, others will tolerate only a few special knots.

Ropes are typically made using one of two different processes. The most traditional – twisted rope – has a spiral appearance. It's made from at least two strands of material that are wrapped in opposing directions (to prevent them from unwinding). Such rope can be made quickly from rougher materials – either by hand or using simple machinery – and so they tend to be cheaper.

It is possible to splice twisted ropes together. Braided ropes are the more modern kind, and are quite common today. They require more sophisticated machinery to create them, as the fibre bundles weave over and under each other to create a tight tubular braid. There are several different ways to braid rope; some have a filler core or twisted strands as a centre. Braided rope is far more durable under friction, and when made from synthetic materials (as it often is), this rope fares better in the elements. The only real drawback with braided rope is that it cannot be spliced.

**QUICK TIP:**

*When made from synthetic materials, the cut ends of a rope can be melted to prevent unravelling. This is not without risk, however, as sharp edges can occur, and these can slice your hands if the rope slips through them. Binding cut ends with tough tape or string whipping is preferable.*

## NATURAL ROPES

In former times, natural ropes were the only choice. Their main benefits are sustainable manufacture and ease of disposal (they biodegrade quickly). Their main flaws include vulnerability to UV light, mould, mildew and moisture. These ropes also tend to shrink and stiffen after getting wet, making tight knots almost impossible to untie.

**Cotton:** Soft cotton fibres are spun into yarn and braided into cotton rope that is usually earmarked for a light-duty purpose, such as a clothesline. It is not suitable for heavy loads, friction or sudden shocks. Cotton rope is the only natural rope that is commonly braided, while most other natural ropes are twisted.

**Jute:** This natural rope tends to have a shaggy texture. Small jute cord is often three-ply, but thicker products are available. Jute is often used for crafts rather than practical applications, although many survivalists carry a small section of jute cord for fire making. Cut into short lengths, jute unravels easily to leave loose fibres that make great fire-starting tinder.

**Manila:** Sometimes mistakenly called 'hemp' rope, manila rope is made from the abaca plant – a banana relative grown for its fibre in the Philippines. Tougher than cotton or jute, manila is durable enough for farmwork, camp craft and landscaping, but it can be rough on the hands.

**Sisal:** This rope is made from the fibre of an agave plant species that is native to southern Mexico. Today, the plants are commercially grown in many countries, and the strong fibre is commonly turned into twine for hay bailing on farms. Sisal rope is more resistant to salt water than some other natural ropes.

**Hemp:** This very soft, flexible rope is made from industrial hemp. It's also stronger and more rot-resistant than most other natural ropes. For these reasons, hemp rope was heavily used during the age of sailing ships – from the top of the sail rigging to the bottom of the anchor rope.

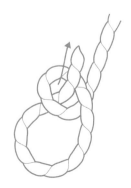

## SYNTHETIC ROPES

Synthetic ropes can be made from several different raw materials and assembled in a variety of ways. You'll find several different braids available in synthetic ropes (with or without a core). You'll also see a few twisted ropes made from synthetic. The main benefits of synthetic rope are strength, rot resistance, and utility around water.

**Polypropylene:** This lightweight rope is great around the water. Mildew-resistant and rot-proof, some polypropylene ropes also float. Commonly used in boating and commercial fishing, this is also one of the cheaper rope materials. The only drawbacks are that it can stretch, UV light will damage it and friction can weaken it quickly.

**Nylon:** With superior strength and stretchiness, nylon rope is often used for hauling, lifting and tying things down. This smooth rope is resistant to friction and stronger than polypropylene. It's also UV-resistant. Most climbing ropes are made from nylon. It is, however, better suited for dry land, since it readily absorbs water and becomes heavy when wet.

**Polyester:** A great general-purpose rope, polyester resists rot, abrasion and UV light. Often mistaken for nylon, it is commonly used in the outdoors and around the water.

**Kevlar:** Invented in 1965, Kevlar has been used to make fireproof cloth and bulletproof armour. It also makes a rope that is (gram for gram) stronger than steel. Kevlar makes the strongest rope and won't weaken in extremely high temperatures. It also resists freezing, cuts, chemicals, stretching and abrasion. The only real drawbacks are that it is expensive and it does weaken with constant sun exposure.

# MAKING A ROPE

You can only carry so much gear in your backpack, and if you've ever spent time being self-reliant, you'll understand just how alarming it can be to get down to your last coil of line. Thankfully, today's world is full of strong and versatile synthetic materials that can be twisted into rope, as well as natural ones.

## Gather Some Material
One of the most common natural rope materials is the inner bark of certain trees. You can even use long hair, dried animal sinews, strips of leather and stretched dried intestines. Finally, from the modern world, you could cut strips of cloth or plastic to twist into rope. There are plenty of choices – your materials simply need to be strong, flexible and long.

## Start Twisting
Machines can twist any number of fibre strands into a rope, but when twisting a rope by hand, a two-ply twist is the most reasonable. The process is often called 'reverse wrapping', as each ply twist is accompanied by a reverse twist of the overall rope.

### HOW TO TWIST
**1.** Take a long bundle of plant fibres and hold it one-third of the way from one end. This will give you a 'short leg' and a 'long leg' of fibre.

Begin to twist the short section, holding the fibre firm in your left hand and continuing to increase the twist with your right hand. I usually work in a clockwise direction, but you could go either way. After a few twists, the fibres will naturally want to kink and form a little loop. Allow this to happen.

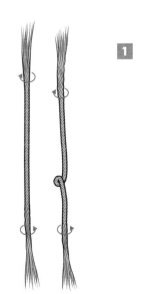

**2.** Pinch the newly formed loop between the thumb and index finger of your left hand. Your short leg should be about one-third of the fibre-bundle length, and the other side would naturally be two-thirds of the length.

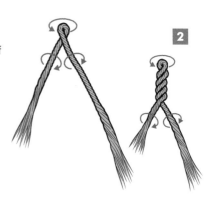

Remember how you started? Let's say it was clockwise. Grab one of your bundles (long leg or short leg) and give it one twist clockwise (about 180 degrees). While holding the tension, flip the other fibre bundle towards you, wrapping it anticlockwise around the bundle you just twisted clockwise.

**3.** Keep the two fibre bundles oriented so that you have one bundle upwards and one downwards (12 o'clock and 6 o'clock). Now continue your twisting pattern. Twist the 12 o'clock bundle clockwise and flip the 6 o'clock bundle towards you and then up, into the 12 o'clock position.

**4.** Keep it up, always twisting the 12 o'clock bundle clockwise and flipping the 6 o'clock bundle forwards and up. Advance the pinch grip of your left hand, so that the thumb and index finger stay right where all the action is happening, at the crossing of the two fibre bundles. Before you know it, you'll have a length of two-ply rope hanging out of your left hand.

**5.** Once you approach the end of the 'short leg' of fibre, make a new bundle of fibre that has the same girth. Spread the fibres at the end of each bundle (cut each one to a tapered point for best results). Now push the fibre bundles together to form a splice. Dampen the spliced area with water, if the fibres don't stick together naturally.

**6.** You should always stagger your splices, as the intact fibres of the long leg form a bridge over the splice, adding strength to the area. Keep adding fibre bundles of the same girth in the same way – that is, when one 'leg' runs out – and keep twisting rope until you have the length you need or run out of fibre. Tie an overhand knot (see page 20) in the end of the rope or create a whipping (see page 137) to keep your new rope from unravelling.

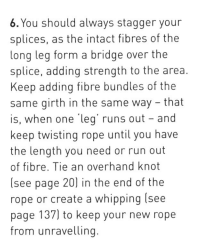

# KNOT TERMINOLOGY

For the best understanding of this complex subject, and before embarking on any knot tying yourself, it will help to know the main groups of fastenings and the proper terms.

### KNOTS, BENDS, HITCHES AND LASHINGS

**Knot**: A knot is any kind of fastening made using loops of rope (or a flexible, rope-like material). A true knot generally ties onto itself to create a fastening in a solitary rope. Knots generally keep their shape once tied, even when they are not under tension.

**Bend:** A bend is a knot that typically secures one rope to a second rope – for example, to make a longer rope. Bends also keep their shape once tied.

**Hitch:** A hitch is a fastening made between a rope and some other object. Most of the time, hitches are tied to logs, sticks, poles, posts and rings. These types of fastenings may slide or be fixed in place, depending on the type of hitch. Hitches don't typically hold their form when they are not wrapped around something or are under tension.

**Lashing:** Similar to a hitch, a lashing is typically used to secure two or more objects together. Lashings are more complex than hitches and require more rope. Most lashings are used for the purpose of building something.

## TERMS FOR KNOTS, BENDS AND HITCHES

**Working end:** This is the end of the rope that is actively being used to tie the knot.

**Standing line:** This is the section of rope that is not active in the knot-tying process. The 'standing end' is at the very end of the standing line, and so furthest away from the working end.

**Loop:** The basis of so many knots and fastenings, a loop is a closed circle of rope.

**Turn:** A turn is one pass of the rope around an object (like a post) or through an object (like a ring).

**Bight:** A bight is a 'hairpin' turn anywhere on a rope. It is not a loop, because it doesn't cross over itself. Instead, both sides of a bight stay parallel to one another.

**Dressing:** This is the act of straightening, equalizing and adjusting a knot, hitch or lashing prior to setting it.

**Setting:** This is the act of tightening a knot. Without proper setting, your knot can be loose and it may even fail. Always make sure a knot is properly dressed before setting it.

## TERMS FOR LASHINGS

**Wrappings:** Loops made around the outside of the objects you are fastening together.

**Frappings:** Loops that encircle the wrappings. Frappings are a necessary component of lashings, providing extra strength and rigidity to the binding. They run between the separate objects you are securing, but outside of your wrappings. When pulled tight, the frappings compress the wrappings and tighten your lashing significantly.

**Racking turns:** These are frappings used in tripod lashings. They run perpendicular to the wrappings and between the sticks or poles.

## TERMS FOR GENERAL ROPECRAFT

**Splicing:** This is the act of untwisting the ends of two ropes and meshing them to each other. Splicing enables you to join two ropes together or to create some new rope feature such as an eyelet.

**Kernmantle:** Meaning 'core-sheath', a kernmantle rope is made from a braided polyester sheath (the mantle part) that encases a unidirectional nylon core (the kern part). These ropes are typically used in rescue operations and recreational climbing.

# 01

# KNOTS YOU NEED TO KNOW

**Overhand Knot**

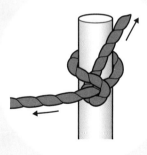

**Two Half Hitches**

**Half Hitch**

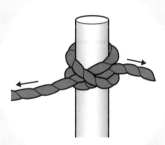

**Clove Hitch: Over the Top**

It's hard to build anything of importance without a solid foundation, and learning to tie knots is the same way. Without a strong grip on the basics, the more complicated knots in this book will be overly difficult to learn and frustrating to practise. The first eleven knots, bends and hitches in this

**Clove Hitch: Around a Tree**

**Figure Eight**

**Square Knot**

**Bowline**

book may seem rudimentary, but it's a mistake to skip over these first knots. Yes, some of the knots in our first chapter may be simple, but that doesn't mean they are unimportant. These are some of the knots you'll use most often, and they form a vital foundation for many of the fastenings to come. In my wilderness camp, you'll see sheltering tarps held overhead by sheet bends in their corners (after the storms

**Bowline on a Bight**

**Sheet Bend**

**Double Sheet Bend**

**Rolling Hitch**

have ripped the metal grommet rings out). You'll see cut ropes rejoined by the reef knot, bowlines used for a variety of tasks and overhand knots tied in the ends of almost every rope or cord as stoppers (and to keep them from unravelling). These first eleven knots aren't the beginner knots at the start of the book. These are the knots you'll find yourself using over and over again.

# OVERHAND KNOT

## THE SIMPLEST KNOT FOR A STOPPER

This is an easy knot to get you started, and it's so useful. It's tied more often than any other knot. You can tie overhand knots in the ends of cut ropes to prevent unravelling during camping use, or add them to the working end of a rope when tying other knots.

**HOW TO TIE**

**1.** Create a single loop near the end of a rope.

**2.** Wrap the working end of the rope around the outside of the loop and pass it through the loop.

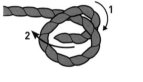

**3.** Pull the working end and standing end of the rope to set the knot.

### USES FOR THE OVERHAND KNOT

• It's one of the simplest stopper knots you can use as 'insurance' on other knots. First, tie the more complex knot, then tie an overhand knot in the working end of the rope – as close to the first knot as possible.

• In the event that the complex knot starts to slip, the overhand knot will hit the side and prevent the slipping knot from creeping any further. While there are bigger and better stopper knots, few can be knotted so quickly and cinched so closely against another knot.

# HALF HITCH

## THE BUILDING BLOCK FOR NUMEROUS HITCHES

While a single half hitch won't reliably hold anything, it's an important foundation for more complex knots, making them very strong and reliable.

### HOW TO TIE

**1.** Wrap the working end of the rope around a post, ring, tree or other object. The rope should cross over itself, making a complete loop.

**2.** Taking the working end in hand, form a second loop around the standing end of the rope.

**3.** Slide the second loop tightly against the object, inside the half hitch.

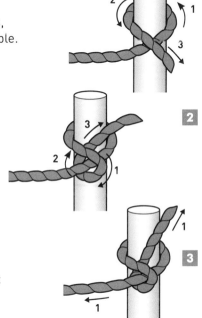

### USES FOR THE HALF HITCH

• The most important use for this hitch is as a building block for other hitches.

• A single half hitch, even in a thick rope with a high-friction texture, just won't hold much. It is often used to hitch a horse (that has no intention of leaving) to a hitching post. The fastening is more psychological than physical for the animal. If the horse thinks it is tied, it won't even try to pull on the rope.

# TWO HALF HITCHES

## A STURDY WAY TO ATTACH A ROPE TO A POST OR STAKE

You can stack half hitches in multiples and add other elements to create a hitch that is secure and sturdy. This version of two half hitches involves adding a 'round turn' for extra strength.

### HOW TO TIE

**1.** Begin this hitch with the round turn element: wrap the working end of the rope around a post or similar object once, as if making a half hitch. Continue in the same direction to wrap the working end of the rope around the object a second time.

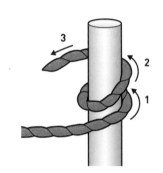

**2.** Make a first half hitch: wrap the working end of the rope around the standing end to create a loop that spirals back towards the post. Dress the hitch.

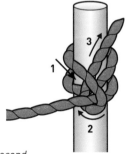

### QUICK TIP: EXTRA SECURITY

*Once you've secured two half hitches, repeat the second one to add a third. This acts as an insurance policy, and is useful when building survival shelters or hanging home-made hammocks. An overhand knot tied in the working end, and snug against the second half hitch, will have the same effect (see page 20).*

**3.** Now add a second half hitch around the standing end of the rope, working in the same direction as the first half hitch.

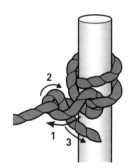

**4.** Dress so that the two half hitches are snug against each other, and then set the hitch tightly. If you worked the hitches correctly, the side view should resemble a clove hitch (see page 24) wrapped around the standing end of the rope.

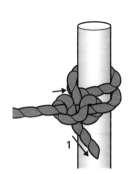

## USES FOR TWO HALF HITCHES

• This hitch is useful for setting up tents and tarp shelters; tied around a tree or a stake in the ground, it can weather storms.

• Adding a round turn allows you to hold tension on a rope while tying the hitches. This is helpful in sailing – when securing a mooring line, for example – with the round turn taking some of the strain.

• If using a hoop through which the rope is too thick to pass through twice, tie two or more half hitches without the round turn.

# CLOVE HITCH

## A TEMPORARY HOLD ON A LOG, TREE OR POST

Also known as a double hitch, the clove hitch is quick to tie and easy to untie. It is best used for non-load-bearing tasks and is not recommended for securing people or property.

### HOW TO TIE OVER THE TOP
**1.** When you can reach over the top of a post or the end of a log, create a loop in the working end of the rope and slide it down onto the post.

**2.** Create a second, identical, loop. For example, if the first loop spiralled clockwise and down the post, make the second one to match. Slide the second loop over the top of the post.

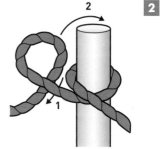

**3.** Dress the hitch and set it tightly.

### QUICK TIP: BEST PRACTICE
*The overlapping part of this hitch should be on any side of the post other than that facing the direction of the load. For example, if the rope is being pulled south, the overlapping part of the hitch should be on the north, east or west. If tied on the south side, the rope will pull the overlap apart and the hitch will release.*

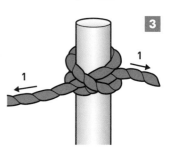

## HOW TO TIE AROUND A TREE

**1.** When you cannot slide a loop over the top of an object such as a tree trunk, wrap the working end of the rope around the object.

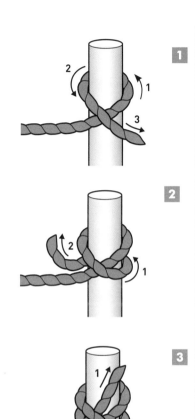

**2.** Wrap the working end around the object a second time, below the first loop, and tuck the working end up and under the loop you just made.

**3.** Dress so that the loops are spaced on one side of the object, and with the working and standing ends of the rope touching and running parallel to each other where they overlap on the opposite side of the object.

**Warning:** While this hitch holds tolerably in rough, natural rope, today's slippery synthetic ropes are not a reliable match. This makes the clove hitch dangerously weak when used incorrectly.

### USES FOR THE CLOVE HITCH

• The most reliable use for the clove hitch is when working with lashings (see pages 60–67). Lashings secure poles and other objects to each other, and the clove hitch is a common starting point for these fastenings.

# FIGURE EIGHT

A FAST, NON-BINDING STOPPER AND THE BASIS OF OTHER KNOTS

Also known as a Flemish knot and a savoy knot, the figure eight makes a fine, single-stranded stopper knot. It is the basis for a family of knots that are commonly used in climbing and rescue work.

**HOW TO TIE**
**1.** Form a bight at one end of the rope and twist the end of the bight to make a loop. It can be clockwise or anticlockwise.

**1**

### USES FOR THE FIGURE EIGHT

• In sailing and climbing, the figure eight makes an easy-to-tie stopper knot for the end of a rope and is easier to untie than a tightly bound overhand knot.

• Once you know the figure eight by heart, it becomes easier to tie climbing and rescue knots such as the figure-eight follow-through knot (see page 94).

**2.** Wrap the working end around the standing end to form a second loop.

**3.** Now bring the working end up through the first loop. The knot will resemble the figure '8'.

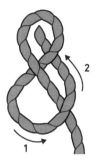

**4.** To set the knot, pull the standing end and the working end simultaneously and in opposite directions.

## QUICK TIP: LOOKING GOOD

*If it doesn't look like an '8' before you set it,*
*go back a step and see what went wrong.*

# SQUARE KNOT

## A QUICK, STRONG WAY TO JOIN MATCHING ROPES

Technically a bend, and often referred to as a reef knot, the square knot is a simple way to join two lengths of matching rope.

### HOW TO TIE
**1.** Create a bight in the working end of rope one. It should resemble the letter J. Hold your bight flat, as if it were lying on a table.

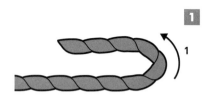

**2.** Take the working end of rope two and pass it up through the bight from below.

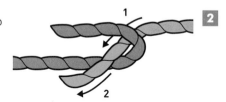

### QUICK TIP: GRANNY KNOT
*If the ropes aren't parallel coming out of this knot, with the short working ends on the same side, you tied something other than a square knot. Many people routinely take a wrong turn on the second part of this knot and create a granny knot, with the short working ends sticking out perpendicular to the standing ends.*

**3.** Make a turn around the entire bight. You can work in a clockwise or anticlockwise direction.

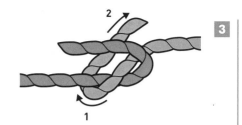

**4.** Run the working end of rope two back down, over the working end of rope one and through the bight. Pull the ends of both ropes in opposite directions to set the knot.

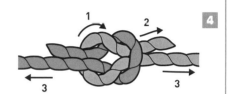

**Warning:** Only use this knot for tying ropes of the same diameter and texture, otherwise use a sheet bend (see page 34). Do not use a square knot in climbing or similar settings, as it is not as reliable as other rope-joining bends.

### USES FOR THE SQUARE KNOT

• This is a good choice for combining two matching ropes to create a longer one, or for rejoining a cut rope.

• You can also use this knot to join the ends of a short rope – for example, around a bundle of firewood, or similar, for easier carrying.

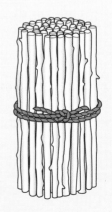

# BOWLINE

## A STURDY LOOP AT ONE END OF A ROPE

The bowline is useful in situations where you need a secure loop at one end of a rope. The loop can be set for any size you need.

**HOW TO TIE**

**1.** Create a small loop towards the working end of the rope, but allow enough excess in the working end to form the size of fixed loop you need.

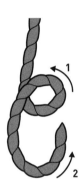

**2.** Run the working end of the rope up through the small loop.

**QUICK TIP: THE RABBIT STORY**

*Here's a way to memorize the bowline. Make a hole in front of a tree (the first loop). A rabbit (the working end) comes up out of the hole, hops behind the tree (the standing end) and goes back down the hole. Then a giant (you) pulls the tree out of the ground. You hold the knot with one hand as you pull on the standing end with the other.*

**3.** Wrap the working end around the standing end and insert it back down through the small loop.

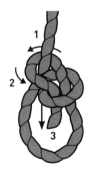

**4.** Dress so that the knot lays flat and resembles an upside-down sheet bend (see page 34). Pull the working and standing ends in opposite directions to set the knot.

## QUICK TIP: PRACTICALITIES

*It isn't practical to tie this knot while holding a heavy weight on the standing end. Once tied, however, a bowline can come undone if left without a load on the standing end. It can also work loose if tied using stiff rope.*

### USES FOR THE BOWLINE

• A bowline can be tied quickly and thrown out to struggling swimmers.

• Slipped over a post or a stake, a bowline can secure watercraft and shelters.

• You can use two bowlines to link two ropes together. Tie them one after the other, interlocking the loops like chain links.

# BOWLINE ON A BIGHT

## A BOWLINE WITH A DOUBLE-STRANDED LOOP

The bowline on a bight allows you to create a strong, slip-resistant double-stranded loop in the middle of a rope where there is no access to the working end.

### HOW TO TIE

**1.** Draw out a long bight in the rope and tie it off using a very loose overhand knot (see page 20).

**2.** Keep the overhand knot loose enough to make the desired size of fixed loop. Open the bight.

### QUICK TIP: ALTERNATIVE KNOTS

*The bowline on a bight isn't the only loop you can create in a rope where there is no access to either end. The figure eight directional loop (see page 26) and alpine butterfly loop work just as well (see page 96).*

**3.** Now flip the opened bight around the entire overhand knot.

**4.** Cinch the bight closed around the parallel standing ends to make the fixed loop and set the knot.

### USES FOR THE BOWLINE ON A BIGHT

• The extra loop here can provide additional grip when used as a rescue knot.

• The two loops could be formed with a large circumference and separated to grip different areas on someone's body (such as the thighs and chest). Smaller loops could provide a secure handhold or foothold.

• This double loop can also be used for hitching in situations where the loops don't need to tighten.

# SHEET BEND

## AN EFFECTIVE WAY TO JOIN TWO DISSIMILAR ROPES

This knot is a 'bend', since it joins two separate ropes together. While most bends work best when joining two ropes of equal thickness and similar texture, the sheet bend can join very different thicknesses and qualities of rope.

### HOW TO TIE

**1.** Identify your thicker rope and create a bight at the working end. The bight should resemble the letter J. Hold the bight flat, as if it were lying on a table.

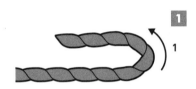

**2.** Take the working end of your smaller-diameter rope and pass it up through the bight from below.

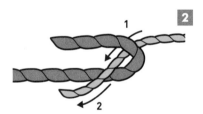

**3.** Make a turn around the entire bight. You can work in a clockwise or anticlockwise direction.

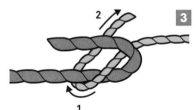

### QUICK TIP: EXTRA INSURANCE

*Tying a stopper knot in the end of your smaller-diameter rope will ensure that this bend doesn't slip apart.*

**4.** Tuck the working end of the smaller rope under itself, on top of the bight.

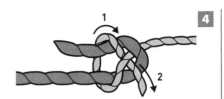

**5.** Dress the sheet bend by pulling lightly on the two standing ends, then pull harder to set it.

### USES FOR THE SHEET BEND

• This bend can connect two ropes that have no business being able to hold on to each other – for example, to connect thumb-thick rope to very skinny lines, when accompanied by a stopper knot.

• Rope isn't the only thing a sheet bend can grab. You can also use it to tie a rope to the corner of a piece of fabric or tarp. Simply take the corner, squeeze it into a rope-like shape, and fold it into a bight. This can come in handy when creating an emergency shelter and the grommets on a tarp are torn out, absent or too small for the rope diameter.

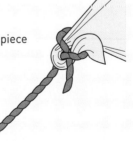

• You can tie sheet bends in two corners of a piece of fabric to hoist it as a signal flag.

• The uses for camping, bushcraft and survival are numerous.

# DOUBLE SHEET BEND

## A MORE SECURE VERSION OF THE BASIC SHEET BEND

When a single sheet bend doesn't feel solid enough – say, when tying a tarp for shelter or in an emergency – the double sheet bend adds extra grip and security.

### HOW TO TIE

**1.** Take the thicker rope, bundle of fabric or the corner of a tarp, and create a J-shaped bight at the end. Hold the bight flat as you would a regular sheet bend.

**2.** Pass the working end of the smaller rope up through the bight.

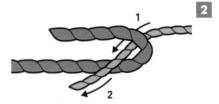

**3.** Wrap the working end around the entire bight two times.

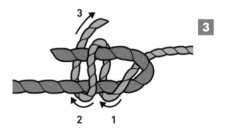

### QUICK TIP: EXTRA INSURANCE

*If you're concerned enough to tie a double sheet bend, add a stopper knot (see page 48) to the working end of your slender rope, too. Cinch it tight against the dual wraps.*

**4.** Pass the working end under the two wraps, on top of the bight.

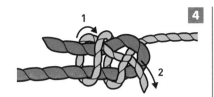

**5.** Dress the double sheet bend by pulling the standing ends, adjusting the two wraps, and pulling the working end snug. Apply the load slowly to set the knot and compress the bight.

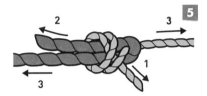

**Warning:** The double sheet bend can join almost anything to almost anything. You can use it when building shelters, though it has a long history of nautical use too. Like anything else, however, there are limits. When the smaller line is too small, this bend may not hold.

### USES FOR THE DOUBLE SHEET BEND

• Like the basic sheet bend, this type of fastening can join radically different diameters of rope and allows you to join rope to materials other than rope – from clothing to plastic tarp.

• The double sheet bend provides better security than the standard sheet bend, with very little extra rope required.

# ROLLING HITCH

## A SLIDE-AND-GRIP HITCH THAT ADDS AN EXTRA 'LEG' TO ROUGH-TEXTURED ROPE

The rolling hitch has been used in sailing and dogsledding for centuries. Over the years it has also been known as the magnus hitch and Magner's hitch. Suited to rough rope, it allows you to tie an extra 'leg' to a rope under tension. The rope used for these extra legs is typically more slender than the main rope.

### HOW TO TIE

**1.** Using a thinner rope, wrap the working end around the rope under tension. Leave a good length of working end for further wrapping.

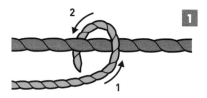

**2.** Wrap the working end a second time, crossing over the first loop. As you come around, bring the working end to the left of the standing end.

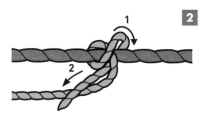

### QUICK TIP: ALTERNATIVE KNOTS

*Even in rough, natural rope, this hitch won't hold unless it is pulled parallel to the rope or pole to which it is tied. For a perpendicular pull, use the alpine butterfly loop instead (see page 96).*

**3.** Wrap the working end a third time. This time, as you come around, bring the working end to the right of the standing end and tuck the working end into the loop you have just made. The two loops to the left of the standing end run in the direction of pull, while the third loop runs in the opposite direction.

**4.** Dress the hitch so that the three loops are stacked tightly against each other, and set the hitch tightly.

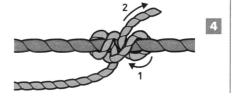

**Warning:** This hitch is unreliable when using synthetic rope. If tying extra legs onto a slick rope, use an icicle hitch.

### USES FOR THE ROLLING HITCH

• The rolling hitch can be used to connect additional elements to a main rope or pole, as long as they pull parallel to it.

• This hitch can also be used as part of an anchoring system or to relieve some of the weight of a loaded line.

• The most interesting aspect to this hitch is the fact that it can slide when it's not under a load. Simply take the load off your line, slide the rolling hitch up or down the main rope as needed and apply the load again. The hitch will pull a slight angle in the main rope, thus allowing the hitch to grip.

# 02

# CAMPING AND HIKING KNOTS

**Jam Knot**

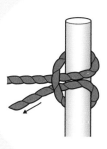

**Cow Hitch**

**Stevedore Stopper Knot**

**Timber Hitch**

While the average outdoor enthusiast may be able to muddle through their adventures by learning only two or three knots, the more educated outdoor fanatic knows better. They know that learning how to tie a wide variety of knots will give you a wider range of options out in nature. These added options are particularly important when you are providing for your own needs in the wild. The more knots you know, the more

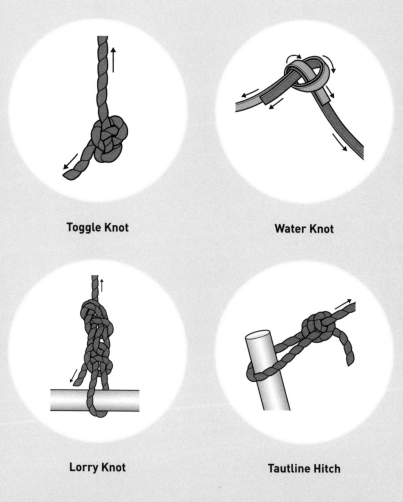

**Toggle Knot**

**Water Knot**

**Lorry Knot**

**Tautline Hitch**

options you will have when attempting to accomplish your daily tasks. Whether you're stretching out a tarp to create a shelter or building a more complicated structure with poles and lashings, these camping and hiking knots can provide you with more than just variety during your daily chores. These knots can provide greater security and safety (and even comfort) to those who call the wilderness 'home'.

**Diagonal Lashing**

**Shear Lashing**

**Tripod Lashing**

**Square Lashing**

In this chapter, you'll learn eight great knots and hitches that are useful on the trail and in camp. You'll also learn how to create four different lashings, which will enable you to build camp objects from poles and rope. With the foundation of handy knots you learned in chapter one, it's time to build upon the most commonly practised knots and add even more to your bourgeoning skill set.

# JAM KNOT

## A TIGHTENING HITCH FOR BUSHCRAFT AND FISHING

The jam knot is often called the Canadian jam knot when used in bushcraft and camping, and is identical to the arbor knot used in fishing. It's actually just a pair of overhand knots used in tandem.

**HOW TO TIE**
**1.** Run the rope around the object or bundle you intend to secure.

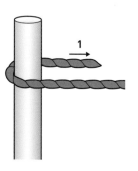

**2.** Use the working end to tie an overhand knot (see page 20) around the standing line.

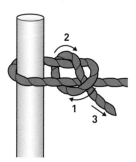

**QUICK TIP: EXTRA FRICTION**
*When using the jam knot to connect a fishing line to the slick spool in a fishing reel, some anglers make a few round turns around the spool for extra friction.*

**3.** Tie a second overhand knot in the working end of the rope, close to the first overhand knot.

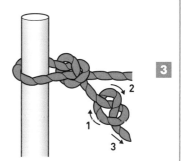

**4.** Tighten both overhand knots so that the first one is tight against your object and the second is tight and snug against the first.

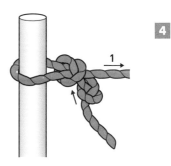

### USES FOR THE JAM KNOT

• When used in the mountains and woods, the jam knot can be a great choice for compressing gear and supplies. It works well when bundling sticks for firewood, for example, or when rolling up a foam sleeping pad.

• Some bushcrafters also use the jam knot to start lashings when connecting poles together.

• Around the water, the jam knot is handy for connecting a new section of fishing line to a spool.

# COW HITCH

A SIMPLE HITCH TO BIND A ROPE WITH A LOAD TO A POST

This hitch has a long history and has gone by plenty of names, including ring hitch, dead-eye hitch, lark's head hitch, lanyard hitch and even lark's foot hitch. Essentially, it's a clove hitch with the second loop made in the reverse direction to the first. It holds better than a clove hitch, especially when the tension of the load is likely to change directions.

### HOW TO TIE

**1.** Create a loop around the post, rope or other object you intend to fasten your load to.

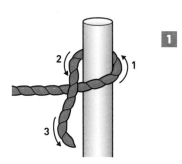

**2.** Take the working end of the rope over the standing end before wrapping the working end around the object again – this time in the opposite direction. Leave a bit of slack.

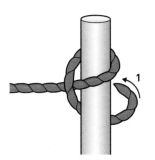

### QUICK TIP: EYE LOOPS

*For webbing or a strap with an eye loop at one end, you can tie a cow hitch by wrapping the eye loop around an object and threading the standing end through the eye loop. This can be useful for dog leads and other gear.*

**3.** Slide the working end under the slack to complete the hitch. Dress the hitch so that the working end and standing end are side by side. Pull both ends to set the hitch.

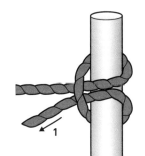

**Warning:** Like the clove hitch (see page 24), the cow hitch is not known for great strength. To improve this, tie it with a bight in the middle of a rope and secure both loose ends. Even then, this hitch is not recommended for heavy-duty loads.

### USES FOR THE COW HITCH

• In rope, this hitch can be used instead of a clove hitch for a more reliable fastening.

• In our agrarian past, farmers used this hitch to tie a cow to a post or tree for grazing. Even if the animal walked around the post repeatedly, the hitch would hold (unlike a clove hitch, which can fall apart when the tension of a load changes direction).

• The name 'lanyard hitch' also hints at a practical use: using a loop of cord, the hitch can be made by threading a bight from the loop around an object and threading the loop through the bight.

• When used with straps or webbing, the hitch is called a 'girth hitch'.

# STEVEDORE STOPPER KNOT

## A MIDSIZE STOPPER KNOT

Stopper knots come in single-strand and multistrand varieties. For this book, we have chosen the stevedore stopper knot. It's not the fattest stopper knot in the world, but it's quick to tie and should seem familiar. It's like a figure-eight knot, but with an extra loop from the working end.

### HOW TO TIE

**1.** Create a bight at the working end of your rope.

**2.** Wrap the working end around the standing end two times.

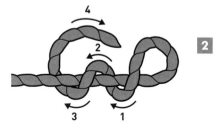

### QUICK TIP: BEST STOPPERS

*Dozens of different knots can act as stoppers. They keep a knot or hitch from slipping undone, they prevent the cut end of a rope from unravelling and they can simply offer something for you to grip. See also the overhand knot (page 20) and figure eight (page 26).*

**3.** Take the working end of the rope back through the bight. Dress the knot, stacking the loops closely together.

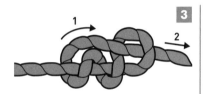

**4.** Now pull the working end and standing end in opposite directions to set the knot.

**Warning:**
Depending on the slipperiness of a synthetic rope, other stopper knots may be more secure than this one.

### USES FOR THE STEVEDORE STOPPER KNOT

• The main use for any stopper knot is to prevent a rope from slipping past a certain point. In the days of tall ship sailing, this knot was used to prevent a rope from slipping through pulleys. Today, it is used in tandem with other knots, hitches and lashings to secure them.

• This knot can also keep a cut rope from unravelling, prevent a rope from slipping through your hands and act as a weight for tossing the end of a rope.

• Use this midsize stopper knot to secure a tarp by running a rope through each grommet and tying the knot on the rear side.

# TIMBER HITCH

A WAY TO FASTEN A ROPE TO A LOG

Historically used by loggers to allow draught animals to drag logs from woodland areas, the timber hitch is a quick way to fasten a rope to a log, tree or other cylindrical object.

### HOW TO TIE

**1.** Start by making a turn around the log or object with the working end of your rope. If you're tying it to a log on the ground for the purpose of dragging the log, tie the hitch near the end of the log. Prop the log up, if necessary, to be able to reach underneath it. Once around the log, make sure you have enough slack on the working end of the rope to wrap back onto itself for a small distance.

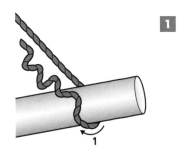

**2.** Pass the working end of the rope around the standing line, keeping plenty of slack, and back towards you.

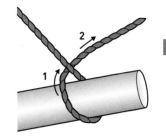

### QUICK TIP: BEST ROPE

*This hitch grabs best and is most reliable when tying it with thicker, softer, squishier rope. This is because the rope can compress and conform to uneven bark surface on a log.*

**3.** Now spiral the working end around itself four or five times. It should look like a twisted eyelet, with the standing line coming through it.

## 3

**4.** Dress the hitch by snugging it up against the log and equalizing the spiral wraps of the working end. Set the hitch by pulling it tight. You're now ready to put weight on the line!

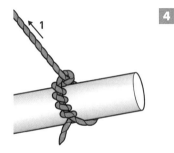

### USES FOR THE TIMBER HITCH

• If you ever need to drag a log through the woods – pulled by a truck, a mule or yourself – the timber hitch is a great choice. It's ideal for gripping rough cylindrical objects.

• The timber hitch is also a popular way to start a diagonal lashing (see page 60), as the initial fastening holding the two poles together.

• If using the hitch to begin a square lashing (see page 66), tie it to just one of the logs or wooden poles and not around both.

# TOGGLE KNOT

## AN ELONGATED 'BUTTON' AT THE END OF A ROPE

A toggle knot forms a button or toggle at the end of a rope. You can think of it as an overgrown stopper knot. Here's just one of many ways to tie a single-strand version.

**HOW TO TIE**

**1.** Create two bights near each other and near the end of your rope.

**2.** Thread the last bight on the rope through the adjacent bight.

**QUICK TIP: COLOUR CODING**

*If you wish to make more complicated multistrand toggle knots, try starting out with different rope colours woven into a toggle. The separate colours help your eye track the pattern and make the knot a little easier to tie.*

**3.** Pass the working end of the rope through the threaded bight and around the last bight in the rope.

**4.** Pass the working end through the end of the threaded bight, and dress the knot by removing all slack.

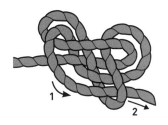

**5.** Pull the working end and standing end to set the knot.

**Warning:** This is not a load-bearing knot and should not be used as such.

### USES FOR THE TOGGLE KNOT

• The most obvious use is to employ this knot as a button or toggle.

• There are dozens of different toggle and button configurations. Some are single-strand knots, as here, while others rely on multiple strands of rope to create complex woven patterns. Typically, the more complicated the design, the more likely the knot is to be decorative rather than functional.

# WATER KNOT

A GOOD WAY TO JOIN TWO PIECES OF WEBBING, STRAPS OR BELTS

Flat materials are hard to fasten together, which is why it is important to add the water knot to your repertoire. Actually a bend, it is ideal for joining two separate materials together. While commonly used in webbing, it can also join belts and straps of the same width. Its configuration should seem familiar to you, as it is based on the overhand knot. Different names for the water knot include tape knot, ring bend and grass knot.

**HOW TO TIE**

**1.** Create a very loose overhand knot at the end of one piece of webbing.

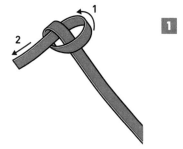

**2.** Thread the working end of the second piece of webbing through the overhand knot – starting at its working end.

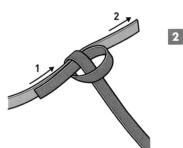

**3.** Thread the second piece of webbing along the exact path of the overhand so that it comes out alongside the standing end of the overhand knot. Dress the knot by equalizing all parts, and set the knot by pulling the standing ends in opposite directions.

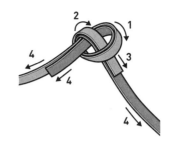

**Warning:**
For security, make sure you have at least 8–10 centimeters (3–4 inches) of working end hanging from each side of this knot. You'll also want to make sure that your webbing, belts or straps stay flat while tying and while in use. This bend is not reliable if the webbing begins to roll up or take on a tubular shape.

### USES FOR THE WATER KNOT

• The best use for the water knot is for joining two matching pieces of flat material together. In all cases, both pieces should be of equal width and thickness.

• While this bend is used in climbing, keep in mind that it isn't a perfect knot. Should the outer piece of webbing become caught on something, it could pull the knot apart.

# LORRY KNOT

## A HITCH THAT CAN TIGHTEN AND SECURE

Likely pre-dating the internal combustion engine and going back to an era of horse and wagon, this hitch is also known as trucker's, haymaker's and harvester's hitch. It creates a lightweight pulley system without needing the traditional block-and-tackle gear. It makes use of several components to offer a mechanical advantage when tightening a load. It also offers a way to secure itself after tightening.

### HOW TO TIE

**1.** Create a bight next to a loop in your standing end, leaving plenty of rope on the working end to loop back and forth.

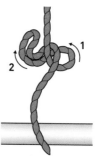

**2.** Bring the bight over the standing end of the rope and down through the loop, to create a directional figure-eight knot.

### QUICK TIP:

*This hitch can be tied with other loops instead of the directional figure eight, but certain knots can cause a problem. After a heavy load has been applied to the hitch, certain knots can be set so tightly that they cannot be untied. The directional figure-eight knot is both secure and easy to untie, even after holding a heavy load in transport.*

**3.** Run the working end around your anchoring object and then thread it through the figure-eight loop. Pull your load as lightly as you need and hold the tension.

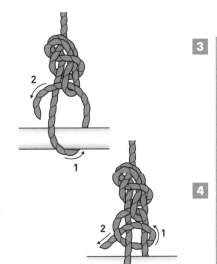

**4.** Add two or three half hitches (see page 21) below the loop to finish the hitch.

**5.** Dress the half hitches snugly against each other and pull the working end tight to set the knot.

### USES FOR THE LORRY KNOT

• If you happen to drive a lorry, you'll see the value of this hitch right away. It takes the place of mechanically tightened straps for securing a load to a vehicle.

• It's also handy on watercraft and around camp. Whether securing tarps or loose objects, the rope threading back and forth acts as a pulley and allows you to secure the rope more tightly than you could without the mechanical advantage.

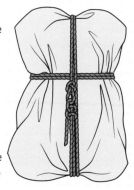

# TAUTLINE HITCH

A SLIDING KNOT THAT GRIPS UNDER TENSION

For those who camp under tents and tarps, half of the battle in pitching your shelter is the adjustment of your rainfly or outer covering. Tighten one line and another goes loose or becomes too tight. Tent manufacturers try to help by providing a variety of slide-and-lock mechanisms on tent guy lines – but what can you do when you don't have those? The answer is the tautline hitch.

**HOW TO TIE**

**1.** Run the working end of the rope around the tree, stake, ring or other object that you intend to use as an anchor point.

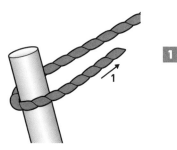

**2.** Wrap the working end around the standing end twice, spiralling in the direction of the anchor object.

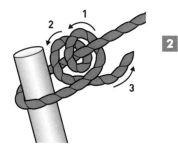

**3.** Bring the working end away from your anchor object and add a third loop around the standing end.

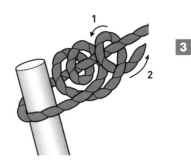

**4.** Dress the knot by constricting it and snugging the three loops tight against each other. Set the knot by pulling the working end and sliding the three loops to the desired position on the 'taut' line.

**Warning:**
This 'slide-and-grip' hitch isn't recommended for any major loads. It may slide out of position even when under tension, and it will definitely slide when the standing line is not under tension (that's what this hitch is supposed to do).

### USES FOR THE TAUTLINE HITCH

• The tautline hitch is essentially a rolling hitch (see page 38), tied in the same piece of rope, rather than two separate ropes.

• The tautline hitch can replace the sliding lock commonly found on tent lines. Just make sure that the standing end is under a fair amount of tension to make it hold.

• The three wraps pull the standing line on a slight angle, and this little 'zigzag' in the standing line is the secret behind the hitch holding.

# DIAGONAL LASHING

CONNECTS STICKS OR POLES THAT CROSS EACH OTHER AT AN
ODD ANGLE

Lashings are cordage wraps that bind poles, planks, rods and sticks
together. Different lashings are used when building structures such
as shelters and camp furniture, and the diagonal lashing is best for
joining poles that cross each other at an odd angle.

**HOW TO TIE**

**1.** Tie a timber hitch around the two
objects you intend to join.

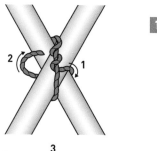

**2.** Wrap tightly around the outside
of the two objects with three or
four passes.

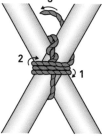

**QUICK TIP:**

*As we have discussed earlier, the clove
hitch is an unreliable hitch to use with slick
modern rope. Most books and instructors
stick to the tried-and-true formula (ending
all lashings with a clove hitch), but I'd
encourage you to choose something stronger. My preference
is to leave a long working end on the hitch that starts your
lashing, then tie off the lashing with a square knot using the
end of the rope.*

**3.** Then wrap the same number of passes around the two objects on the other axis.

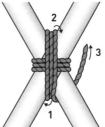

**4.** Add three or four frapping turns around the wrappings. These will go between the poles and around the outside of the wrappings.

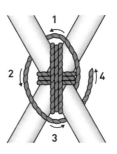

**5.** End the lashing with a clove hitch or any other hitch you prefer.

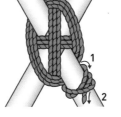

## USES FOR THE DIAGONAL LASHING

• Want to build a watchtower, hut or bridge using rope, sticks and poles? Use the diagonal lashing in any place where two poles cross each other at an odd angle. Diagonal members provide a surprising amount of support in a structure and prevent square and rectangular shapes from losing their shape.

# SHEAR LASHING

HELPS CREATE A LONGER POLE FROM TWO OR MORE
SHORTER LENGTHS

When you need a long pole but only have short ones available, you may think you're out of luck. But with the shear lashing, you can join poles and sticks to each other – until you run out of rope. This is the way to tie this odd but useful lashing.

**HOW TO TIE**

**1.** Start by tying a clove hitch (see page 24) around one of the poles.

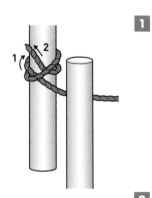

**2.** Wrap around the outside of both poles four or five times, but not as tightly as you could, as you'll need enough room for frapping between the poles.

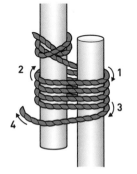

**QUICK TIP:**

*If you're attempting to make a very long pole from shorter pieces, use two short shear lashings per joint. The pair will actually hold better than one long shear lashing (since a long continuous wrapping tends to stretch).*

**3.** Now make two or three very tight frapping turns around the outside of the wrappings you made in step 2, but between the poles.

**4.** Finish the lashing with a clove hitch or something stronger (see Quick Tip, page 60).

### USES FOR THE SHEAR LASHING

• This lashing may seem like it's only good for turning short sticks into a longer stick, but it can also work in a different way. By securing the ends of two sticks, you can open the sticks up like scissors (likely the reason for the name 'shear' lashing) and create an 'X' with two long legs.

• This could be a structural member, for shelters and other constructions. You could also use it as a free-standing bipod for a variety of purposes. The shear lashing can make long poles or a pair of scissor-like legs.

# TRIPOD LASHING

## CREATE A TRIPOD FROM THREE POLES AND SOME ROPE

The numbers don't make sense, but the effectiveness is undeniable. Three legs are better than four when it comes to stability. The tripod lashing allows us to quickly create shelters and many different camp items, using the structural stability of the triangle.

### HOW TO TIE

**1.** Begin by laying three poles on the ground, side by side. Tie the hitch of your choice to the right or left pole – the traditional clove hitch is used here (see page 24).

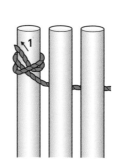

**2.** Wrap around the outside of all three poles. Do this four or five times – not too tightly, as you'll need room for the frapping turns between the poles.

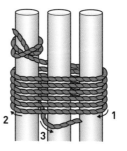

**3.** Create your frappings by encircling the wrappings between the poles. Frap twice between each pair of poles. Work back towards your original hitch to tie off on its working end, or hitch to a free pole space on the opposite side of the lashing (as shown here).

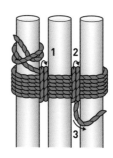

**4.** Complete the lashing by tying a hitch or knot to secure the frappings. You can now spread the tripod legs to stand it up.

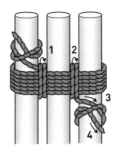

**Warning:**
While the tripod is a very stable structure, it can still fall if you don't strive for symmetry in construction and placement. Each of the three legs should be the same length and similar in diameter. When standing upright, the spacing between the three legs of the tripod should w be equidistant. The legs should be spread out wide enough to prevent the tripod from toppling over, yet not spread so wide that it can collapse flat.

## QUICK TIP: HIGH-TENSION OPTION

*Some bushcrafters tie their tripods with the centre pole pointing in the opposite direction to the two outside poles. The ropework is the same, but when the tripod is set up, the central leg must flip over, adding extra tension to the lashing in the process.*

## USES FOR THE TRIPOD LASHING

• This might just be one of the most versatile lashings you can create in your camp. Tripods can be large or small. A huge one could be the basis of a conical shelter, such as a teepee. Midsize tripods make great cooking rigs to hold pots and food over a fire.
• Your imagination is the only limit here – how about using a small tripod with some horizontal cross pieces added as a drying rack to make jerky?

# SQUARE LASHING

## CONNECTS STICKS OR POLES THAT CROSS EACH OTHER AT RIGHT ANGLES

Best used when joining two poles that are at right angles to one another, when tied properly, the square lashing offers rigid support to any structure you wish to build.

### HOW TO TIE

**1.** Start by tying the rope to one of the poles, close to where they cross each other. The clove hitch is a traditional choice, but a square knot or jam knot (see pages 28 and 44) is more effective. The square knot is shown here.

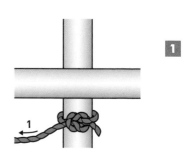

**2.** Wrap the rope in a spiral around the two poles four or five times, passing under the lower pole and over the top pole.

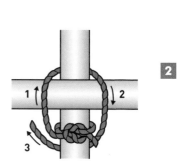

### QUICK TIP: TIGHT WRAPS

*For a tighter pull on your rope as you create wrappings and frappings, wind your rope around a short, strong stick and use it as a toggle to pull the rope harder than you could pull it using your bare hands. This technique can be used for fastening almost any knot, hitch or lashing, but is especially useful to constrict the longer sections of rope that lashings require.*

**3.** Now create a tight frapping by passing around the outside of the wraps, but between the two poles, three or four times.

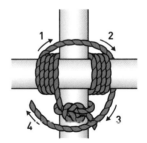

**4.** Once the frappings are tight, use your preferred hitch or knot to secure the end of the rope. The clove hitch (see page 24) is shown here.

## USES FOR THE SQUARE LASHING

• This lashing is typically the most useful when it comes to building in camp. You can build shelter frames, racks, benches, beds and other furniture items from stout poles and strong rope.

• This lashing has also been used for far more elaborate projects, including towers and bridges.

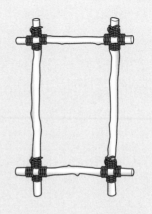

# 03
# NAUTICAL KNOTS

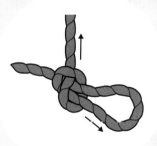

**Slip Knot**

**Cleat Hitch**

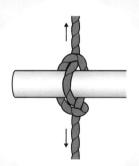

**Marlinspike Hitch**

Few of history's knot users are as iconic as the sailor. With a mastery of wind, water, tide and rope, the sailors of olden days explored the world and opened new trade routes, laying foundations for the world we know today. None of this travel and trade would have been possible without the myriad

**Anchor Hitch**

**Ashley's Stopper Knot**

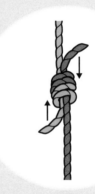

**Double Fisherman's Knot**

knots that held those ships together and helped the crew to perform the vital tasks needed for a life on the water. Today, unlike the tall ships of old, we may not have miles of rigging on our watercraft, but we still need ropes and knots on the water. Whether your vessel is powered by the wind in its sails or is fuelled by the diesel in its engines, you'll still

**Figure-eight Fisherman's Knot**

**Granny Knot**

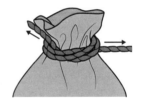

**Strangle Knot**

need to know how to handle the ropes and tie reliable knots. In this chapter, you'll learn nautical knots and hitches from recent times as well as a number of knots that date back to antiquity. Don't be tempted to skip over these knots if you live a landlocked life. These fastenings aren't just useful on the water – they can be used almost anywhere.

# SLIP KNOT

A SIMPLE STOPPER KNOT THAT FEATURES A NOOSE

Very similar to the jam knot, the slip knot creates a quick and simple noose for a variety of chores aboard the ship (and on dry land). The main component of this knot is the overhand knot.

**HOW TO TIE**

**1.** Create a loop in your rope, far enough from the working end to yield the noose size you require. Pass the working end through the loop to create a loose overhand knot (see page 20).

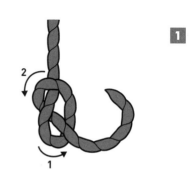

**2.** Now run the working end back through the centre of the overhand knot, leaving the desired noose size.

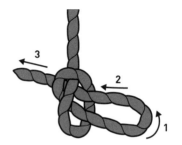

**3.** Pull the standing end of the rope and the bottom side of the noose to tighten the overhand knot and complete the slip knot.

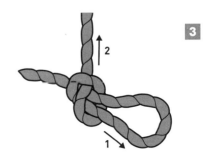

**Warning:** The slip knot is just that, and can easily 'slip' apart. Do not use it to create a load-bearing loop or noose.

### USES FOR THE SLIP KNOT

• While it's not as rugged as the jam knot (see page 44), the slip knot can still tackle many jobs. It is used as a non-jamming stopper knot, which can be untied easily by pulling the working end (when nothing is inside the noose).

• This knot has been used on watercraft for centuries to secure loose objects.

• On land, the slip knot can be used as a trap component (though the jam knot would make a far better snare noose).

• Slip knots are even used in knitting and crochet work.

# CLEAT HITCH

A KNOT FOR SECURING A ROPE TO A CLEAT

A common fixture around docks and watercraft, a cleat is shaped a little like an anvil and bears two symmetrical horns. While you'll occasionally see a cleat in a dry setting, no other fastening methods are as traditionally nautical as this.

### HOW TO TIE

**1.** Pass the working end of your rope around the far side of the cleat. Run the rope beneath both 'horns' but do not make a full turn (loop) around the waist.

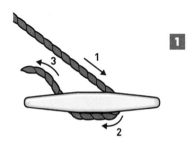

**2.** Wrap the working end of your rope over the top of the cleat and under each horn in a figure-eight pattern.

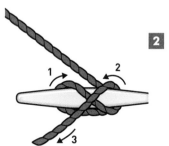

### QUICK TIP: EXCESS ROPE

*Once the hitch is complete, you may have a long section of rope left over. Coil this neatly at the base of the cleat. This is called 'flaking' a rope. The rope is still underfoot, however, and adds nothing to the strength of your hitch. A different option is to secure the excess working end rope to the standing line using a rolling hitch (see page 38) or some other sliding hitch. With the extra rope out of the way, it's almost impossible for the cleat hitch to come undone.*

**3.** Repeat this figure-eight wrapping at least two times, depending on the thickness of your rope and the size of the cleat.

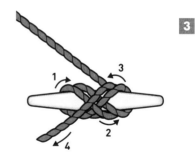

**4.** Finish the cleat hitch with a half hitch (see page 21).

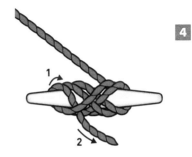

**Warning:** If you are likely to need to release the cleat hitch quickly, skip the half hitch in step 4, as this may take too long to untie.

### USES FOR THE CLEAT HITCH

• There's just one basic use for a cleat hitch, and that's to secure a rope to a cleat. The most common usage for the hitch is when tying off a vessel to a dock.

• You may also use this hitch to connect two small vessels with a rope for towing.

• Away from sailing vessels, you will also commonly find a cleat hitch on a flagpole.

# MARLINSPIKE HITCH

## A HITCH FOR SECURING A ROPE TO A ROD OR POLE

The name of this hitch is believed to derive from 'marling' – the practice of whipping a thin twine around the cut ends of thicker rope and wrapping twine overtop of rope splices. A pointy spike was often used in this craft and it was known as a 'marling spike'. Over the years, the name of the hitch was shortened to 'marlinspike'.

**HOW TO TIE**
1. Create a loop in your rope.

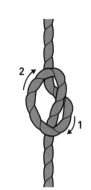

**1**

2. Pull a bight of the standing line through the loop.

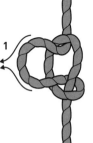

**2**

### QUICK TIP: BEST PRACTICE
*Check this hitch often and retighten as needed – it's only a temporary hitch. There is a 'right' and 'wrong' direction to tie the marlinspike hitch when making a rope ladder or handle. The 'crossing' of the original hitch loop should be below each ladder rung, as demonstrated. If this crossing is above the rung, the hitch can slide during use. When used as a handle, the loop crossing should be towards the person pulling, not towards the load that's being pulled.*

**3.** Insert a pole, rod or other object through the bight.

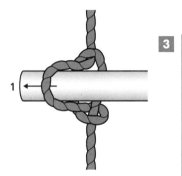

**4.** Pull the rope on each side of the hitch to tighten the bight around the pole or rod.

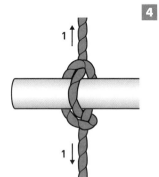

**Warning:** When making a ladder, never use slick-surfaced poles or pole sections that are too narrow for your body width. It's possible that either of these deficiencies could cause a rung to be pulled or pushed out of position – particularly when you are hanging from it.

## USES FOR THE MARLINSPIKE HITCH

• Used for a variety of outdated ship's tasks in the past, today the most interesting application for the marlinspike hitch is in creating a rope ladder. With a series of these hitches – and some good, strong poles – you can quickly create a temporary ladder for use on your vessel or dry land.

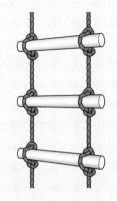

• This hitch can also be used at one end of a rope (or anywhere along its length) to insert a rod that can act as a handle, providing the user with a stronger grip on the rope.

# ANCHOR HITCH

A HITCH FOR TYING A ROPE TO AN ANCHOR, POST OR PIER

This hitch shares a strong resemblance to two half hitches with a round turn (see page 22). It also shares the same functionality, though there are some structural differences.

## HOW TO TIE
**1.** Loosely wrap the working end of the rope twice around the object to create a round turn.

## QUICK TIP: EXTRA SECURITY
*If using this hitch to secure something important (such as your one and only anchor), consider adding some insurance to your hitch – an extra half hitch or two around the standing line, for example. If you're tying the hitch to a post and you have some extra working end, tie it to the standing line using a rolling hitch (see page 38). This gets the excess line off the deck and adds more security to your anchor hitch.*

**2.** Bring the working end over the standing end of the rope and up through the round turn.

**3.** Tie a half hitch around the standing line. Dress the hitch before setting it tightly.

## USES FOR THE ANCHOR HITCH

• This hitch is used to secure an anchor line to iron anchors, hence the name.

• It can also be used to secure ropes to posts, trees and many other structures.

• Sometimes called the fisherman's bend or hitch, it 'anchors' a rope in place with the same security as a round turn and two half hitches.

# ASHLEY'S STOPPER KNOT

A CLASSIC NAUTICAL STOPPER KNOT

This knot is named after Clifford W Ashley. One of the greatest knot historians of all time, Ashley wrote the *Ashley Book of Knots* over a 10-year span and after much research. Published in 1944 and containing much lore and almost 4,000 fastenings, it remains an invaluable reference for all knot-tying aficionados.

**HOW TO TIE**

**1.** Start by creating a bight and folding it forwards to make two loops. The loop closest to the standing line should be the larger of the two.

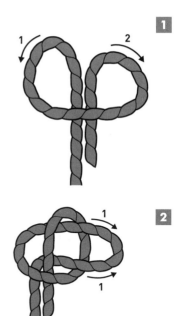

**2.** Bring the larger loop from the standing line side through the smaller loop on the working end side.

**QUICK TIP: RELIABLE STOPPER**

*While this knot is a little trickier to tie than a figure eight, it's worth the trouble. It's more secure than a figure eight and many other stopper knots – so long as it's tied correctly.*

**3.** Draw the smaller loop tight and pass the working end up through the larger loop.

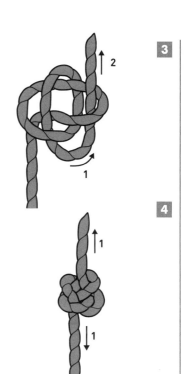

**4.** Pull the working end tight and then pull the standing line tight.

**Warning:** If you don't tighten the components of this knot in the correct order, it will not form correctly. Your finished product should be symmetrical and beefy with three equal 'lobes' visible from underneath. If it doesn't look like that, untie it and try again.

### USES FOR THE ASHLEY'S STOPPER KNOT

• This fat stopper knot is easy to tie and makes a great addition to the working end of a rope that may otherwise slip through your hands.

• While Ashley calls this knot the 'oysterman's stopper', it's commonly named in his honour. Had it not been for his life's work, this knot – and countless others – would be lost to us.

# DOUBLE FISHERMAN'S KNOT

## A TIGHT-SETTING BEND TO JOIN SIMILAR OR MATCHING ROPES

Technically a bend, the double fisherman's knot is a fastening that can join two matching or very similar ropes together. It's also called the double Englishman and the grapevine knot, likely due to the swollen joints that some grapevines grow.

### HOW TO TIE

**1.** Bring the two working ends side by side, coming from opposite directions.

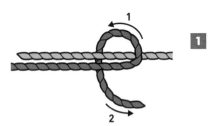

**2.** Wrap the working end of the left rope twice around the standing end of the right rope. Tuck this working end under both wraps.

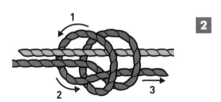

**3.** Dress this first knot by tightening the wraps.

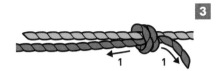

### QUICK TIP: SAFETY FIRST

*For modern kernmantle ropes (such as those used for climbing), choose a bend from the climbing chapter for the best and safest fastening of this type of rope. The sheath-and-core construction of kernmantle may allow the core to slip when using the double fisherman's knot – even if the outer sheath doesn't move.*

**4.** Repeat the two wraps with the working end of the right rope around the standing end of the left rope. Dress and set this second knot.

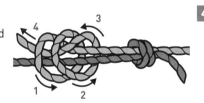

**5.** Pull the standing lines in opposite directions to set the bend, sliding the two sets of wraps together.

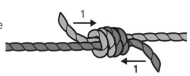

**Warning:** When climbing or hoisting a load, make sure to leave the working ends a little long as they exit each side of the knot. This allows a greater margin of safety for the bend to compress under a heavy weight.

### USES FOR THE DOUBLE FISHERMAN'S KNOT

• This compact knot is a reliable way to join two ropes together using a relatively low-profile bend.

• The best aspect of this bend is that it's relatively easy to tie and easy to inspect for correctness. Each side of the bend should be a perfectly matched strangle knot.

• The downside of this bend is that it compresses so tightly that you may have to cut the rope instead of untying it.

# FIGURE–EIGHT FISHERMAN'S KNOT

JOINS TWO MATCHING ROPES WITH A THREE-PIECE FASTENING

This bend takes advantage of the combined strength of the figure eight and the fisherman's knot. A doubled figure eight is at the heart of the knot, while a matching pair of fisherman's knots brings extra security and keeps stray working ends out of the way.

### HOW TO TIE

**1.** Tie a figure-eight knot (see page 26) in the first rope – near the end but not at the very end. Bring in the second rope towards the figure eight.

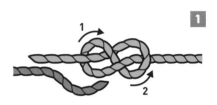

**2.** Slide rope two into the figure eight and follow the path made by rope one to create a second figure eight.

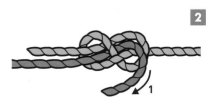

### QUICK TIP: VERSATILE COMBO

*For a fastening that absolutely must hold, take the multicomponent nature of this system and apply it to other knots, bends and hitches. For example, a square knot could be tied with a pair of fisherman's knots made from the loose working ends.*

**3.** Bring the working end of rope two out of the figure eight so it runs parallel to the standing end of rope one. Dress the knot and set it tightly, leaving enough rope for a fisherman's knot in each working end.

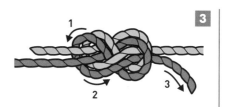

**4.** Tie a fisherman's knot (see page 82) on the working end of each rope. Set all three knots tightly.

## USES FOR THE FIGURE-EIGHT FISHERMAN'S KNOT

• This bend is at home on watercraft, around the docks or even when climbing – it's sometimes used when tying ropes together for top-roping or abseiling, for example.

• Given the extra security of the fisherman's knots, this reliable fastening could join two ropes for heavy work (even if they are not exactly the same size or texture).

• If you need to join two ropes for an anchor line or to tow a small vessel, this one is a solid choice. Note that you may not be able to untie it after taking a heavy load.

# GRANNY KNOT

## A SIMPLE BINDING KNOT

Dating back to antiquity, the granny knot has gone by many names over the years, including false knot, garden knot, lubber's knot, calf knot and booby knot. The knot has long been used to secure bags of milled grain, leading some language scholars to suggest that 'granny' is a corruption of the word 'granary'. In any case, the granny knot is easy to tie and untie.

### HOW TO TIE

**1.** Bring two ropes together, or both ends of the same rope. Tie a half knot, going right over left (or left over right, it's your choice).

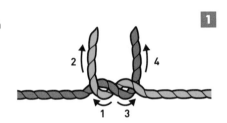

**2.** Repeat step 1 with a second half knot that is identical to the first.

### QUICK TIP: SPOT CHECK

*Many people inadvertently create a granny knot when tying a square knot. In a square knot, the working ends and standing ends should be parallel so that the knot resembles a pair of bights grabbing each other. If your rope ends emerge from the knot in four different directions, making a cross shape, you have tied a granny knot.*

**3.** With the half knots stacked, one on top of the other, alternately pull the standing lines and then the working ends to set the knot.

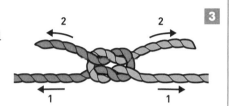

**Warning:** The granny knot looks like a square knot (see page 28), but it has very little of its strength. Do not use the granny knot when any critical load is on the line. As the weight pulls on the standing lines (especially with slick rope), the granny knot can fail.

## USES FOR THE GRANNY KNOT

• The granny knot is quick and natural to tie, since your hands repeat the same motion twice. It should only be used for light-duty tasks, such as tying bags, parcels, packages and bundles.

• Never use a granny for fastening two ropes for climbing or for lashing together any important structures.

# STRANGLE KNOT

### A KNOT TO CINCH UP A BAG OR A HANK OF ROPE

Similar to other constricting knots, the strangle knot can be used to bundle things together and will hold reasonably well in small-diameter twine.

### HOW TO TIE

**1.** Wrap the working end of the rope around the sack, bundle or other object to create a loop.

**2.** Wrap the working end around the item a second time, going below the first loop.

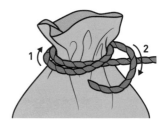

### QUICK TIP: BEST ROPE

*While the strangle knot can be tied in thicker rope, it's better suited to slender lines. The ideal rope for this would be some rough-textured twine. Don't be surprised if a rough line makes this knot difficult to untie.*

**3.** Pass the working end over the standing end of the rope and under the two loops made in steps 1 and 2.

**4.** Dress the knot so that both loops are close together before setting the knot tightly.

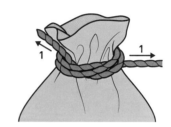

**Warning:** Although this knot is fairly simple, it's also easy to mess up. Pay close attention as you overlap and run the working end beneath the loops.

### USES FOR THE STRANGLE KNOT

• Use a strangle knot to tie the mouth of a bag closed, to bundle up a coil of rope for storage or even as a quick whipping at the end of a thick fraying rope.

• You can use a strangle knot as a light-duty hitch to connect a rope to a pole. Though it's not much stronger than a clove hitch (see page 24) for this purpose, it will hold just fine if tied with a slender line that has a rough surface texture.

# 04

# CLIMBING KNOTS

**Figure-eight Follow-through Knot**

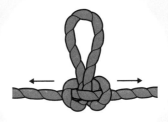

**Alpine Butterfly Loop**

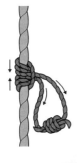

**Prusik Hitch**

**Munter Hitch**

Around your wilderness campsite, it may not matter which knot you choose to bundle your gear or string up a tarp shelter, and it's not the end of the world if that knot fails to perform correctly. Something may fall apart or drop down,

**Super Munter Hitch**

**Bowline Stopper Knot**

**Klemheist Knot**

and everyone may get a good laugh out of it. But in the world of climbing and abseiling, knot tying becomes a far more serious subject. Deadly serious, in fact. Whether a climber is ascending or descending, abseiling down mountains or climbing trees, any knots tied will literally

**Mule knot**

**Figure-nine Loop Hitch**

**Barrel Knot**

have someone's life hanging in the balance. In this chapter, we'll take a look at knots and hitches with great strength and interesting uses, including anchors and abseil knots. All of them can be used for climbing, but you'll find them handy in other arenas as well.

# FIGURE–EIGHT FOLLOW– THROUGH KNOT

## A SECURE LOOP USING A DOUBLED FIGURE-EIGHT KNOT

This fastening creates a sturdy loop using the strength of the figure-eight knot. The loop can be any size you require, making this a very versatile knot.

**HOW TO TIE**

**1.** Tie a very loose figure-eight knot (see page 26) with plenty of extra length at the working end. You need enough to wrap around the object you are hitching and to rethread through the figure eight.

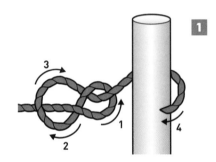

**2.** Wrap the working end of the rope around your anchor point and through the nearest loop of the figure eight made in step 1.

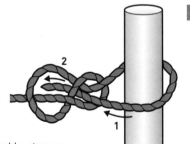

**QUICK TIP: EXTRA INSURANCE**

*Leave plenty of working end hanging, and add a stopper knot for additional insurance. If using the loop to lift a load, you could also fasten the working end to the standing end using a fisherman's knot or rolling hitch (see pages 82 and 38).*

**3.** Continue rethreading the working end through the figure eight.

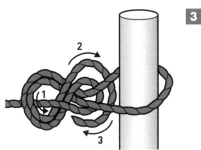

**4.** Finish so the working end exits the knot alongside the standing end of the rope. Dress the knot for evenness, pull it compact (rather than leaving it 'flat'), and set the knot tightly.

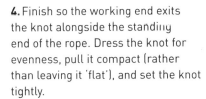

## 4

**Warning:** Easy to tie, this knot is also easy to inspect for safety. If it doesn't look like a doubled figure eight, you'll know right away that you tied it incorrectly. Before putting any weight on the knot, you must be sure to dress it so that the 'outer' parts compress inwards and settle in the most compact form they can take.

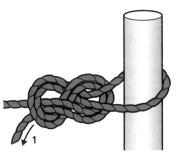

### USES FOR THE FIGURE-EIGHT FOLLOW-THROUGH KNOT

• With a large loop wrapping around a solid tree, this loop can create an anchor point for abseiling in a search-and-rescue situation.

• A small loop can be made for clipping karabiners into when enjoying recreational climbing.

• You could even make a midsized loop to throw to someone floundering in the water.

# ALPINE BUTTERFLY LOOP

A STRONG MID-ROPE LOOP

Sometimes called the lineman's loop (or lineman's rider) due to its use by early telephone and power linemen, the alpine butterfly loop is a common knot among climbers and mountaineers. Slightly resembling a butterfly halfway through the tying process, this knot is a little complex but well worth the time to learn.

### HOW TO TIE
**1.** Working in a clockwise direction, twist two loops into the rope, one above the other. The top loop should be much bigger than the bottom one.

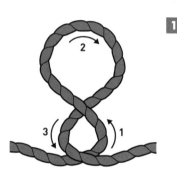

**2.** Pull the bigger loop down over the smaller loop, encircling it.

### QUICK TIP: ROPE DAMAGE
*If your rope contains a nicked or scuffed section but you have to use it anyway, this loop can help you isolate the damaged section. Create the alpine butterfly loop with the worn-out section isolated as the loop component. This removes it from the load-bearing section of the line. Just make sure your fellow climbers know that this loop isn't safe to bear weight.*

**3.** Draw the bigger loop into a shape resembling a bight and pass it up through the underside of the smaller loop.

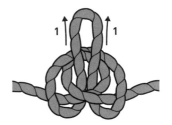

**4.** To dress and set the knot, alternately pull on the 'bight' and each end of the rope.

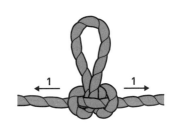

**Warning:** When making this knot, make sure both of the tying loops turn the same way (clockwise). If each loop flips a different direction, the finished knot will be a 'false butterfly' knot. This impostor will look very similar to the real thing, but it will fail under a load.

### USES FOR THE ALPINE BUTTERFLY LOOP

• For climbers, this is the perfect way to add a loop in the middle of a long rope. It is commonly used to connect a climber's harness to the rope, using a karabiner as the connecting link.

• Mountaineers and hikers also use these loops to connect group members to a shared rope when crossing a treacherous area.

• You can use this loop as the integral loop for a lorry knot (see page 56). It holds strong when pulled in either direction on the rope, and is stronger than comparable knots (such as the figure-eight follow-through knot on page 94).

# PRUSIK HITCH

ADDS A LOOP TO A ROPE FOR ASCENDING AND ATTACHMENT

Created by Austrian mountaineer Karl Prusik, the Prusik hitch was developed almost a hundred years ago as a simple tool for rope ascending. It is used for a wide range of purposes today.

**HOW TO TIE**

**1.** Start by creating a loop of slender rope fastened with a double fisherman's knot (see page 82). The loop can have a small diameter or a large one, depending on your purpose.

**2.** Wrap the loop around a second rope and under itself, forming something like a loose cow hitch (see page 46).

**QUICK TIP: ADDED STRENGTH**

*The Prusik hitch demonstrated here has three wraps around the thicker rope, but it can be tied with four or five wraps for added strength.*

**3.** Repeat step 2 twice more, working in towards the centre of the loop.

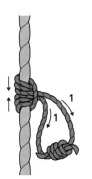

**4.** Dress the hitch so that the wraps stack tightly on the second rope, with the loop hanging from the centre.

**Warning:** This hitch relies on friction. When conditions take away the friction – say the ropes are icy – it is no longer safe. The hitch works best when the loop rope is of a smaller diameter than the rope it is hitched upon. Just make sure it isn't too slender, as this will lower the safe working load that the loop can hold.

### USES FOR THE PRUSIK HITCH

• Going up or going down a rope, the Prusik proves a useful loop that can be large or small.

• Less damaging to rope than mechanical metal ascenders, the Prusik hitch allows a climber to creep up a rope by sliding the hitch upwards (when their weight is off the main rope). The hitch can be used similarly for descending.

• The Prusik hitch can also be used to attach items to a rope, both for climbing and non-climbing purposes.

# MUNTER HITCH

## A QUINTESSENTIAL CLIMBING HITCH

Named after Swiss mountaineer Werner Munter, the Munter hitch is also known as the Italian hitch, flip-flop knot, crossing hitch, tag knot and HMS (short for German *Halbmastwurfsicherung*, or 'half clove hitch belay'). This deceptively basic hitch is a staple for climbers who want a simple belay system. When in use, the wraps create friction and allow the user to control the rate of descent.

### HOW TO TIE

**1.** Make a loop in the rope, with the working end on top of the standing end, and slide it into an open karabiner.

**2.** Create a second loop outside of the karabiner. Again, pass the working end of the rope over the top of the standing end.

### QUICK TIP: ABSEILING

*With solid training and practice, the Munter hitch can also be used for abseiling, though this is very hard on the rope (generating lots of friction) and is generally reserved for emergencies.*

**3.** Slide the new loop into the karabiner.

**4.** Close the karabiner, tighten the hitch and you're ready to belay. Just hold on tight to that rope tail!

**Warning:** With karabiners that have a gate nut that needs hand-screwing to close, keep an eye on that component. It's possible that the friction of the rope rubbing against the knurled surface of the nut can unscrew it, creating an unsafe condition.

### USES FOR THE MUNTER HITCH

• When used as a belay, you don't need any extra gear – just an appropriately shaped karabiner (pear-shaped or at least wide enough for two rope wraps), a good rope and a trustworthy belayer.

• You can also lower loads using this hitch. However you apply it, the hitch can self-regulate. The more weight it has to hold, the tighter the hitch becomes. This tightness generates friction, allowing it to act as a 'brake' on your rope.

# SUPER MUNTER HITCH

## AN ENHANCED VERSION OF THE MUNTER HITCH

For lowering heavy climbers or weighty loads of gear, this upgraded version of the Munter hitch is perfect for the job. It is sometimes called the double Munter or 'monster' Munter.

### HOW TO TIE
**1.** Tie a regular Munter hitch (see page 100) on the 'flat' section of a pear-shaped karabiner.

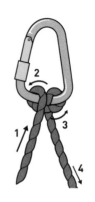

**2.** Wrap the 'tail' of the rope (the part you'll hold) around the loaded side of the rope (the part carrying the weight).

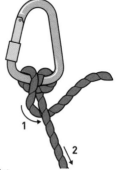

### QUICK TIP: KINK-FREE ROPE
*The regular Munter hitch will sometimes kink or twist a rope with prolonged use. However, the super Munter hitch won't do this, thanks to the extra turn in the rope.*

**3.** Thread the tail through
the karabiner.

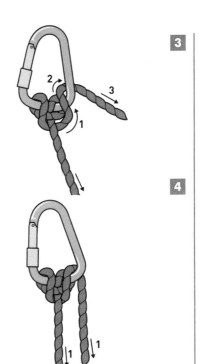

**4.** Dress the knot by moving it to the
centre of the karabiner bottom, and
keep hold of the tail.

**Warning:** If you plan on making
a super Munter from the start,
make sure the tail will be on the
opposite side of the karabiner to
the gate. This prevents the tail from
accidentally unscrewing the nut on
a screw-lock gate.

## USES FOR THE SUPER MUNTER HITCH

• This hitch is primarily applied when lowering
heavy loads, and often used in search-and-
rescue applications. Thanks to the extra
friction, the hitch can hold a lot more weight
than a regular Munter hitch. It simply takes
less muscle to control a heavy descent.

• The only downside is that the extra friction
makes this hitch less useful for normal day-
to-day climbing use.

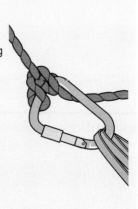

# BOWLINE STOPPER KNOT

## A SOLID LOOP WITH EXTRA INSURANCE

The bowline knot can be used to create a reliable loop that neither opens wider nor closes. While the bowline is reliable, in the world of climbing, nothing can ever be too reliable, so this fastening adds an extra component to increase the knot's natural strength.

### HOW TO TIE

**1.** Begin by tying a regular bowline knot (see page 30), leaving extra length in the working end to create the second knot component.

**2.** Wrap the working end around itself and the side of the bowline loop, in preparation for a fisherman's knot (see page 82).

### QUICK TIP: BEST POSITION

*The fisherman's knot can be placed on either side of the bowline loop, whichever is more convenient. It can even be tied back up on the standing line (outside of the bowline loop).*

**3.** Complete the fisherman's knot, taking the working end through the loops. Dress the knot by compacting the loops and set the knot tightly.

**Warning:** The bowline is trustworthy under most conditions, but the rigours of climbing present a different scenario. It is possible that a bowline can fail in slick rope, particularly if the knot is being thrashed around. For this reason, adding a fisherman's knot to the bowline adds an extra level of security.

### USES FOR THE BOWLINE STOPPER KNOT

• Use this supplemented bowline for rescue work, to fasten to a tree or post or just for regular climbing.

• This familiar hitch is at home around the water, on a cliff side or in your camp.

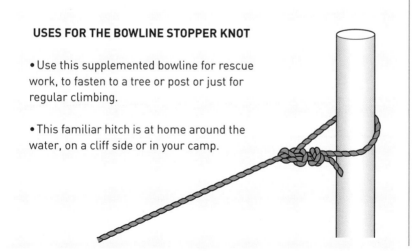

# KLEMHEIST KNOT

## A SLIDE-AND-GRIP KNOT FOR SINGLE-DIRECTION USE

Also called the Machard or French Machard knot, the klemheist is a close cousin to the Prusik knot. The main difference is that the Prusik can work in either direction, while the klemhiest goes only one way.

### HOW TO TIE
**1.** Follow step 1 of the Prusik hitch (see page 98) to create a fixed loop of rope. Now take a bight of the loop and wrap it around a second rope three times.

**2.** Slide the knotted part of the loop through the bight.

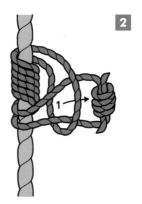

### QUICK TIP: BEST ROPE
*For the Prusik, klemheist and related knots, it's best to make the loop from a rope of a more slender diameter to that of the load-bearing rope. Something in the range of 5 or 6 millimetre (1/4 inch) cord is ideal. The closer the diameter of the loop rope is to that of the load-bearing rope, the less secure these fastenings will be.*

**3.** Dress the knot by pulling on the knotted part to tighten the unknotted bight against the stack of rope wraps. Set it tightly.

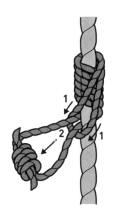

**Warning:** The klemheist is a friction hitch that grabs onto the larger rope when weight is applied to the hitch. If you remove the weight or move the hitch around too much, it can lose its shape. Always inspect the klemheist before putting weight on it.

### USES FOR THE KLEMHEIST KNOT

• Useful in ascending and descending, the klemheist can be used instead of a Prusik for a variety of actions. It's also used occasionally in sailing and arborist work.

• Its structure can vary depending on the slipperiness of the rope it is tied upon. If three wraps don't seem to grip well enough, add a fourth wrap before pulling the loop through the bight.

# MULE KNOT

A KNOT TO TEMPORARILY SECURE A MUNTER OR SUPER
MUNTER HITCH

When using a Munter to belay someone or lower some gear, there
are times when you need to secure the line. The mule knot is a
natural contender for the job. The knot combines a slip knot and
a half hitch.

### HOW TO TIE
**1.** Tie a Munter hitch (see page 100)
around a karabiner and use the tail
to create a loop on each side of the
loaded line. The two loops should
mirror each other.

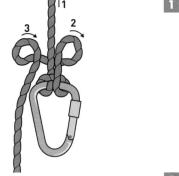

**2.** Pass the second loop you made
through the first loop, and feed
through a little extra rope from the
tail to create a bight. This is the slip
knot component.

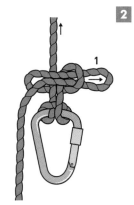

### QUICK TIP: FIRST CHOICE
*The mule knot isn't the only way to tie off a Munter,*
*but it's reliable and easier to untie than some of the*
*alternatives (especially after it has been tightened by*
*a heavy load).*

**3.** Wrap the bight around the back of the loaded line.

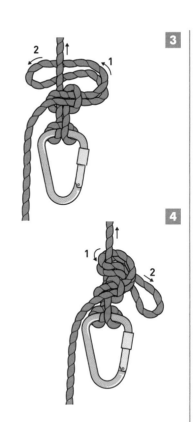

**4.** Now pull the bight under itself to create the half hitch. Dress the knot by compacting all parts and setting it tightly.

**Warning:** A slip knot alone isn't secure enough for this fastening. With the half hitch locking it down, however, the slip knot can't easily slip out of place.

### USES FOR THE MULE KNOT

• The main use for a mule knot is to temporarily secure a Munter-style hitch.

• This non-jamming knot can be tied with a bight, so you don't need the end of the rope to be free, and it's easy to release when it's time to use the Munter for belaying again.

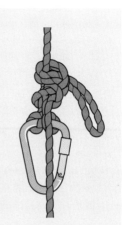

# FIGURE–NINE LOOP KNOT

ONE STEP BETTER THAN A FIGURE-EIGHT LOOP KNOT

Occasionally named the 'figure of nine', this knot creates a rock-solid loop at the end of a rope. Similar to a figure eight, this knot has more strength that comes from an extra half turn. It's not much harder to tie than a figure eight, and it's easier to untie after holding a heavy load.

**HOW TO TIE**

**1.** Form a long bight near the end of your rope and loop it under itself.

**2.** Wrap the bight around the double line, going back the way you came.

**QUICK TIP: BEST ROPE**

*Thanks to the bulkier structure of this loop, it's best suited to smaller and more flexible ropes. A heavy and stiff static line is not a good match for the figure-nine loop. This loop can also be used in webbing material.*

**3.** Pass the bight back underneath everything.

**4.** Thread the bight through the double loop at the end.

**5.** Dress the knot by tightening slightly, and pull the double line and loop in opposite directions to set the knot.

## USES FOR THE FIGURE-NINE LOOP

• Cavers and climbers often use this loop to attach a rope to an anchor point, but it's also handy for any purpose that requires a fixed loop.

# BARREL KNOT

## A THREE-WRAP STOPPER KNOT

Also known as the triple overhand knot, the barrel knot can be a climber's best friend. This big, fat stopper knot can keep your rope from slipping through a belay device if something goes wrong.

**HOW TO TIE**

**1.** Create a loop near the end of your rope, leaving some extra for a 'tail' in the working end.

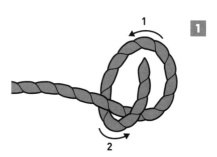

**2.** Make two more loops around the standing end of the rope.

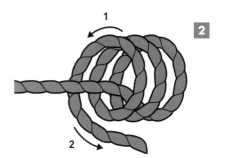

**QUICK TIP: EXTRA SAFETY**

*Make sure that you have more than 45 centimetres (18 inches)*
*of tail hanging out of the end of the barrel knot once complete.*

**3.** Pass the working end of the rope through all three loops and begin to tighten the knot.

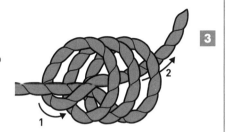

**4.** Dress the knot by stacking and straightening the three wraps. Then, set the knot by pulling the working end of the rope away from the standing end.

### USES FOR THE BARREL KNOT

• The barrel knot can keep a free rope from sliding though belay equipment (or your hands). Essentially, it presents a way to close the system for belaying and abseiling.

• These knots are easy to tie (if you have the end of the rope available), though they can be a little hard to untie after being loaded heavily.

• This knot has a bit of weight from the three loops, and can be used as a weight to toss the rope a short distance.

# 05
# FISHING KNOTS

**Albright Knot**

**Palomar Knot**

**Turle Knot**

In streams and ponds, and in rivers and seas, humans have been catching fish for food and fun for thousands of years. While we still occasionally catch fish using spears and traps, the majority of individuals catch their fish with hooks and line. Formerly, this line was slender string woven from the

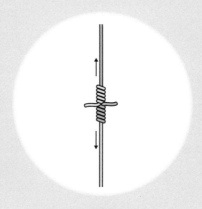

**Blood Knot**

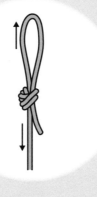

**Double Surgeon's Loop**

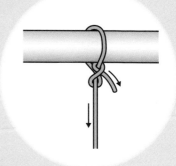

**Buntline Hitch**

strongest plant fibres. Rot-resistant plant fibres were always the most coveted string-making resource, since they could better handle the cycles of being in and out of the water. Today, we can take advantage of the myriad synthetic cords and line that are available to the modern angler, and we don't

**Snell Knot**

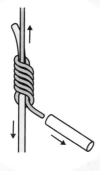

**Nail Knot**

**Improved Clinch Knot**

have to worry about them rotting if they get wet. There's only one problem. Many of these plastic lines won't take the types of knots and fastenings that string will take. And that's why we've dedicated a chapter to the knots you'll need to use with modern fishing tackle.

# ALBRIGHT KNOT

## JOINS TWO DIFFERENT TYPES OF LINE WITH A SLENDER KNOT

In the 1950s, Florida fishing guide Jimmy Albright developed a unique knot for tarpon fishing. Regarded as the 'sheet bend' of fishing line, the fastening allowed anglers to join wildly different lines that were not easily connected using other bends. Still in regular use today, this angling knot is named in Albright's honour.

### HOW TO TIE

**1.** Start by creating a bight in your thicker or stronger material. If using wire leaders, fold the wire into a bight. Pass the smaller line through the bight (from behind).

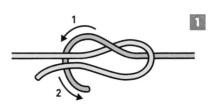

**2.** Give yourself enough extra at the working end of the smaller line to make 10 wraps around the thicker line, working towards the bight.

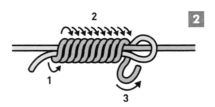

### QUICK TIP: ADDED INSURANCE

*Some fishing aficionados like to add a drop of rubber cement for added insurance on this bend. Adding additional wraps will also strengthen the fastening.*

**3.** Pass the working end of the smaller line though the bight.

**4.** Dress the knot by snugging it up a little, spit on it to lubricate the line (or apply some other non-oily lubricant) and set the knot by pulling it tight. Trim off loose ends.

### USES FOR THE ALBRIGHT KNOT

• If you ever need to join different types of fishing line, this is your bend. It is a solid choice when joining thick, heavy lines and leaders to smaller and lighter monofilament fishing line.

• It's also a popular bend among wire-line trollers, who use the knot to fasten monofilament leaders to wire trolling line.

• It's also a great knot to connect lines to backing material.

# PALOMAR KNOT

## CONNECTS THE EYE OF A HOOK TO A FISHING LINE

Monofilament fishing line is lightweight, strong, rot-resistant and difficult for fish to see, but these assets come at a price. Knots that work well on rope and twine often fail in monofilament. The Palomar is one of several knots that can grip and secure this slippery line.

### HOW TO TIE

**1.** Make a bight at the end of your fishing line, pass the bight through the eye of your fishhook and bring it back over the top of itself.

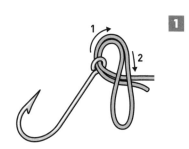

**2.** Thread the bight through the doubled loop in the fishing line, creating an overhand knot.

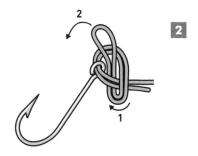

### QUICK TIP: FLEXIBLE CHOICE

*This is an excellent knot to use with both monofilament and braided fishing lines.*

**3.** Thread the entire hook through the bight and bring the bight back up above the fishhook eye again.

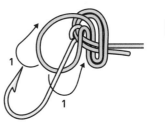

**4.** Snug the knot slightly and spit on it to lubricate the monofilament.

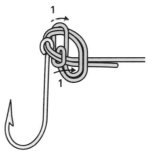

**5.** Pull the standing and working ends of the line to set the knot.

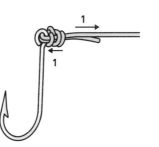

### USES FOR THE PALOMAR KNOT

• You could tie this knot in rope and use it for a variety of hitches on land and sea, but its best application is attaching hook to line.

• Use the Palomar when tying a fly to the tippet of your fly-fishing line (make the bight big enough that it can slip around your fly without damaging any feathers or fibres).

• It's also great for connecting fishhooks to other types of line.

# TURLE KNOT

## THIS HISTORIC ENGLISH KNOT JOINS A HOOK TO A LINE

Mistakenly called the 'turtle' knot on a regular basis, the Turle knot is named after British Major William Greer Turle, a well-known fisherman in the late 1800s, though it's unclear whether he invented the knot or merely popularized it. Easy to tie, this common knot is a great choice for beginners.

### HOW TO TIE

**1.** Pass the working end of the monofilament through the eye of the fishhook and use it to form two loops that are large enough to pass over the hook. Tie an overhand knot around the two loops.

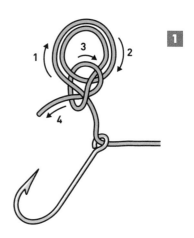

**2.** Bring the pair of loops over the bend of the fishhook and back up the shaft. Pass the working end through the loops and begin to tighten slightly.

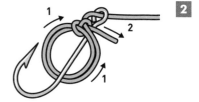

**3.** Spit on the loops to lubricate and set the knot tightly. Trim off excess monofilament after setting it tight.

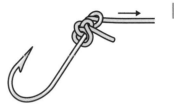

**Warning:** The traditional Turle had a single loop. The thin, strong string fishing line of the 1800s had enough grip to hold a single loop without problem. Today's thin, stiff and slippery fishing lines need the extra loop for security. Tying this knot with just one loop can lead to the loss of both hook and fish.

### USES FOR THE TURLE KNOT

• For connecting hook to line, this knot is a historic favourite. It works well in string and monofilament.

• You can also use it to connect other types of line to an eyelet.

• Need to connect an anchor or grappling hook to a rope? Try the Turle.

# BLOOD KNOT

CONNECTS TWO LINES THAT ARE SIMILAR OR THE SAME

Sometimes called a 'barrel knot', the blood knot is a fishing favourite. This fastening can mend a cut line, or extend a line when longer lengths are warranted.

**HOW TO TIE**

**1.** Bring the two lines parallel to one another. Wrap the working end of line one around line two five times before taking it back and passing it down between the two separate lines.

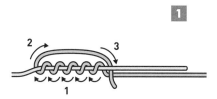

**2.** Wrap the working end of line two around line one five times before taking it back and passing it up between the two separate lines. The working ends of the two lines should point in opposite directions.

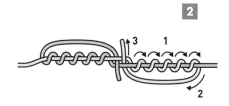

**QUICK TIP: BEST APPLICATION**

*The slender profile of this bend allows it to slide through the water with little resistance, yet it holds with great strength. This makes it the perfect choice when it comes to mending a broken fishing line.*

**3.** Spit on the line to lubricate it and pull the standing ends in opposite directions to dress and set the knot. Trim off excess line to finish.

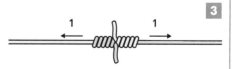

**Warning:** There are several variations of the blood knot (namely, the number of twists and direction of twist). Whichever way you tie it, be sure that the finished knot is symmetrical. While five wraps is the bare minimum you should make, you can increase this to six or seven.

### USES FOR THE BLOOD KNOT

• Perfect for connecting similar line products, the blood knot is excellent for monofilament line. It is a popular knot among fly fishermen, since tippet material can be so tricky to tie.

# DOUBLE SURGEON'S LOOP

## A STRONG LOOP AT THE END OF A MONOFILAMENT LINE

The double surgeon's loop is occasionally called the surgeon's loop or double loop. It's one of the fastest ways to put a secure loop in notoriously slippery monofilament fishing line.

### HOW TO TIE

**1.** Form a long bight at the end of your fishing line and tie it into a large, loose overhand knot.

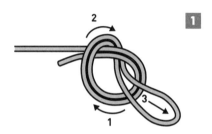

**2.** Wrap the bight around the outside of the overhand knot and back through the centre again.

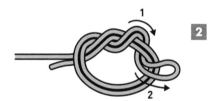

### QUICK TIP: EASE OF USE

*Even though it uses a little more line than other loops, this loop is easy to learn, easy to remember and easy to teach to young and novice anglers.*

**3.** Hold the working and standing ends in the same hand. To set the knot, moisten the line to lubricate it and pull the bight in one direction while pulling the ends of the line in the opposite direction.

## USES FOR THE DOUBLE SURGEON'S LOOP

• This simple fastening offers a quick way to add a loop to the end of your fishing line.

• It's commonly used to connect leaders to the end of a line.

• This loop can be tied in rope or twine for camp or nautical use.

# BUNTLINE HITCH

## ATTACHES A FISHING LINE TO A SPOOL

This knot hails from the days of sailing ships, and was originally used to attach ropes to sails. It can still perform that task, but it can also help to attach backing or monofilament line to a spool.

### HOW TO TIE

**1.** Start by wrapping the working end of your line around the spool, then loop the working end around the standing line.

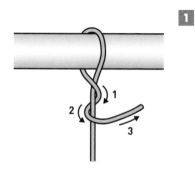

**2.** Pass the working end through the gap created by wrapping around the spool.

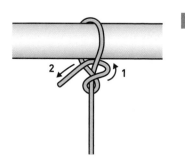

### QUICK TIP: NECKTIE KNOT

*You wouldn't know by looking at it with rope, but the buntline hitch can make a passable necktie knot. It lacks the bulk and symmetry of a double Windsor knot, but it's much easier to tie and untie.*

**3.** Thread the working end under itself and pull the working end to dress the knot. Pull the standing end to set the knot tight.

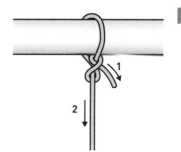

**Warning:** This hitch isn't the most reliable in monofilament line. If using it to connect monofilament to the spool in a fishing reel, try not to let all of your line out, as a fish tugging on the line may cause the hitch to slip. If you want to be ready for a fish that takes all your line, tie an improved clinch knot instead (see page 134).

### USES FOR THE BUNTLINE HITCH

• In addition to connecting monofilament line to a reel, this hitch can be used in rope to connect many different things. For example, you could use it to connect a tent to some tent stakes or tie a weight to a rope.

# SNELL KNOT

## A SHANK WRAPPING KNOT TO ATTACH LINE TO A HOOK

Most early metal fishhooks lacked the 'eye' that we take for granted today, purely because it was difficult for a blacksmith to fashion such a delicate feature. Instead, a hook had a small, round, flattened area at the end of the shank (like a flat spoon). In the absence of an eye, the snell knot was the perfect way to connect a hook to a line. It works equally well on today's modern hooks.

### HOW TO TIE

**1.** Feed the line through the eye of the hook once. Create a large loop before feeding the end of the line back through the eye a second time, and from the same direction.

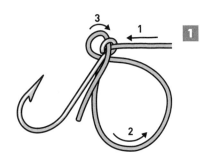

**2.** Twist the side of the loop around the entire hook to wrap the shank.

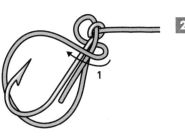

### QUICK TIP: WHEN TO AVOID

*This isn't a great knot choice for 'bait holder' hooks. These have sharp barbs cut into the upper shank of the hook, which do a great job at holding bait (such as insects and chunks of meat), but will likely cut into your tippet or monofilament line.*

**3.** Continue to twist the loop around seven times, holding the wraps tightly with each turn.

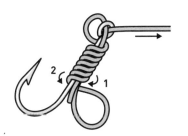

**4.** Dress the wraps for evenness. Spit on the line to lubricate the knot. Pull the standing end and working end to set it. Trim off any excess line from the working end, leaving just a little exposed.

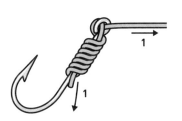

## 4

### USES FOR THE SNELL KNOT

• Once intended for eyeless hooks, the snell knot does an excellent job connecting leaders, tippet or ordinary monofilament line directly to a fishhook.

• This sturdy connection avoids placing extra stress on the line in the way that other knots do. It also lines up the hook shank with your line, which is desirable.

# NAIL KNOT

## CONNECTS TWO FISHING LINES OF DIFFERENT DIAMETERS

Just as the sheet bend allows you to join ropes of different diameters and textures, so the nail knot allows you to connect very different fishing lines. Particularly useful in fly fishing, this common fastening just needs a guide to assist in tying. A short length of plastic drinking straw does the job.

### HOW TO TIE

**1.** Overlap the ends of the two lines you'll be joining and place a short section of drinking straw running parallel beneath them.

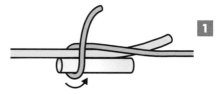

**2.** Wrap the thinner line tightly around the thicker line and straw, making six complete wraps. Pass the thinner line through the straw, tighten the knot a little and pull the straw out of the wrappings.

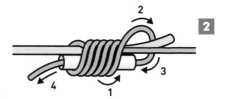

### QUICK TIP: HOLLOW TUBE

*Anglers once used a small nail as a form to wrap around, which could then be pulled out from under the wraps to create a channel for threading the line. These days, a small section snipped from a slender hollow tube, such as a drinking straw, will do an even better job.*

**3.** Lubricate the knot and pull both ends to tighten. Trim off excess line.

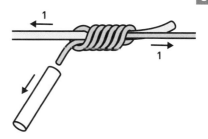

## USES FOR THE NAIL KNOT

• If connecting a thick fishing line to a thinner one, the nail knot has plenty of strength and a low profile that easily moves through guides.

• Use this knot to tie a fly line to a thin tippet piece, or to connect your fly line to the backing.

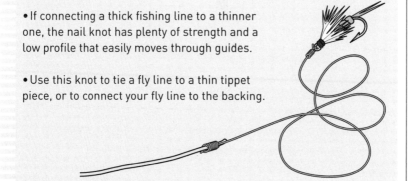

# IMPROVED CLINCH KNOT

JOINS A HOOK TO MONOFILAMENT

For a day of fishing or a lifetime on the water, this could be the only knot you need to know for slippery monofilament line.

**HOW TO TIE**

**1.** Run the working end of your fishing line through the eye of a hook (or around an object). Wrap the working end around the standing line five times and then thread the working end through the wrap closest to the hook eye or object.

**QUICK TIP: FEWER WRAPS**

*This knot becomes harder to tie in heavier line. You may need to reduce from five wraps to four on line that is close to 30 pound test. Choose another knot, such as the Palomar, when tying line that is thicker than 30 pound test.*

**2.** Pass the working end between the wraps and the outer turn.

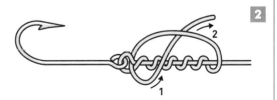

**3.** Lubricate with spit and pull the standing line to set the knot. Trim any excess on the working end.

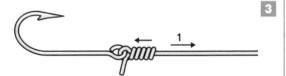

### USES FOR THE IMPROVED CLINCH KNOT

• This versatile knot for monofilament line allows you to tie line to reels, to hooks and to almost anything else you'd need to connect to fishing line.

• You can use a pair of these knots to join two separate pieces of monofilament line.

• This knot is commonly used when connecting line to leaders, swivels, lures and hooks.

# KNOT PROJECT 01

MAKING A WHIPPING

Use small twine as a whipping material to keep large ropes from fraying after being cut.

**HOW TO TIE**

**1.** Lay a bight of twine against the rope, with the curve of the bight at the cut end of the rope.

**2.** Use the standing end of the twine to begin wrapping around both the twine bight and the rope.

**3.** Continue wrapping the twine around the bight and rope until you near the cut end of the rope.

**4.** Pass the end of the twine through the bight and pull on the opposite end of the twine to drag the bight loop under the wrappings. Trim both ends of the twine to finish.

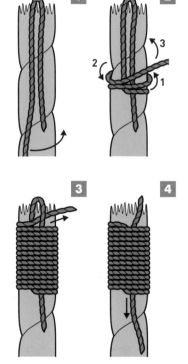

# KNOT PROJECT 02

CREATE A TRIPOD JERKY RACK

Three sticks and a bit of cordage can build a sturdy tripod (see page 64) – a three-legged structure that can be used for dozens of purposes, including a jerky rack, which can suspend salted meat in the smoke of a fire to produce delicious and long-lasting jerky. A modest-sized rack can hold a massive amount of meat, and it's mobile. If the wind changes direction, simply move the tripod to keep it bathed in smoke.

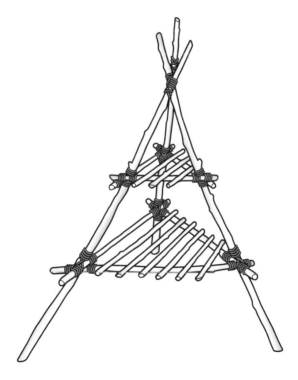

# KNOT PROJECT 03

WEAVE A NET

Nets have been used to catch birds, fish and other animals for thousands of years. It may seem complicated if you've never tried to weave anything before, but it merely requires patience (and a lot of string). Tie a rope between two posts or trees. Using Prusik or cow hitches, hang any number of cords from the rope. Set a guiding string below your rope – this will help you tie net knots in a straight line for even sizing. Tie adjacent cords using an overhand knot and your net pattern will start to appear.

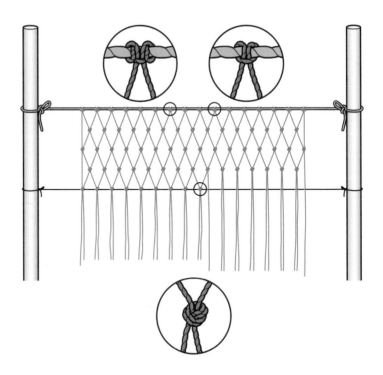

# KNOT PROJECT 04

## BUNDLE YOUR ROPE

Short, long, thin or thick – your rope, twine, cordage and string will treat you far better when bundled for transport and storage. Now that you're done, it's time to put your rope away neatly.

**HOW TO TIE**

**1.** Coil your rope or cordage into an oval coil and wrap the end around the bundle several times.

**2.** Bring a bight of the rope through the bundle.

**3.** Open it up and slide it down over the top of the coil so it sits next to the other wraps.

**4.** Pull the working end to tighten the bight.

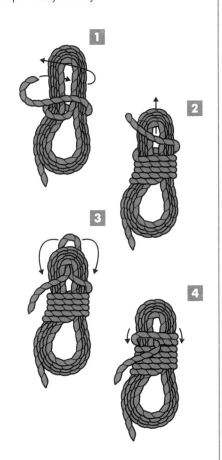

# TRICKS FOR UNTYING KNOTS

You did everything correctly and your knot performed perfectly. It held on tight and did its job. But is the job really done with the success of the knot? Not really . . .

Half of the job is tying the knot, the other half comes when you have to untie it. This can be more challenging than you might imagine, especially after a heavy burden has been applied to the knot and it has constricted to a rock-hard blob. Fortunately, there are a few tricks you can employ to get the knot undone.

## STUDY THE KNOT

The first approach for untying a knot is always to take a good hard look at it to determine what type of knot it is. If you know the knot well, you'll likely remember the last step in tying it, in which case you'll be able to reverse your actions to untie it. If this is not an option and you don't recognize the knot, look for the tail of the working end. Once you have found that, you can progress to the next step.

## TWIST BACKWARDS

Once you have the tail, try backing it into the knot. This is often easier if you apply a tight twist to that section of the rope. The twist stiffens the rope and allows you to push it with greater force. With any luck, the twisted line will slide backwards into the knot and begin to untie it. From there, you can usually just pick it apart.

## STRIKE IT

If the knot hasn't been loaded too heavily, here's a simple trick that can loosen it. Take a spoon or a small hardwood stick and strike the knot several times. Since violent movement can cause a knot to come undone while in use, it's only fair that the same vibration and movement should help it come undone once no longer needed. You don't have to hit the knot with all your might. Just lay the knot on a smooth hard surface and strike it with a series of crisp hits, rotating the knot as you do so. You should find that knocking it around a little will loosen it right up. This may be all you need to do to unmake the knot. If not, try twisting the tail of the working end back into the knot now that you've loosened it up.

## PICK THE KNOT

With a knot that's set hard under a considerable load, you may have one last resort before getting out the knife or scissors. That final hope is picking the knot. Old sailing knives (and even new ones) can be seen with a marlinspike that is very useful for picking knots apart, but these specialized tools aren't the only option. An ordinary corkscrew, a really stout canvas needle, a deer's antler tine and any other thin but strong, object can be used to pick apart a knot. Whatever you choose, just make sure the tip and edges aren't sharp enough to damage your line. To use a pick, find a small gap in the knot, ideally near the working end of the line. Insert your pick and wiggle it in a circle. Make the circle wider as you go and you should start to see the knot loosen. Repeat this in different spots as needed. If all else fails, get your knife out.

# INDEX

# ABOUT THE AUTHOR

**Tim MacWelch** developed a love of the outdoors at a young age, growing up on a farm in the Piedmont hills of Virginia. Since his teens he has been an obsessed devotee of survival and primitive skills. In 1997, he founded the Earth Connection School of Wilderness Survival, which has been featured in *Conde Nast Traveller Magazine* and the *Washington Post*, while Tim personally has appeared on several *National Geographic* programmes, *Good Morning America* and many national news venues.

Tim is the author of seven outdoor survival books, three of which have been *New York Times* best-sellers. He also writes regularly for *Survival Dispatch, Outdoor Life Magazine* and *OFFGRID Magazine*.

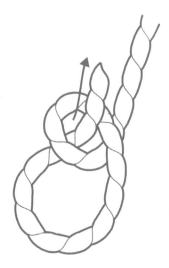